SWIMMING HOLES OF THE OZARKS

A GUIDE TO 85 GREAT PLACES TO COOL OFF IN ARKANSAS AND MISSOURI

GLENN W. WHEELER

WWW.TIMERNST.COM

The photo on the cover was taken at Falling Water Falls in Pope County, Arkansas (see the description on page 44). It's one of the many great cooling-off spots you will find info on inside this guidebook. Swimmers are Alicia Usery, Jesse Scribner, Glenn, Stacey and Beth Wheeler. Photo by Tim Ernst.

Book designed by Tim Ernst, Pam Ernst,
Glenn Wheeler, and Stacey Wheeler
Other Production Team Members:
Judy Ferguson, Norma Senyard

Other guidebooks by Tim Ernst Publishing:

Arkansas Waterfalls guidebook
Arkansas Nature Lovers guidebook
Arkansas Hiking Trails guidebook
Arkansas Dayhikes for Kids & Families guidebook
Buffalo River Hiking Trails guidebook
Ozark Highlands Trail guidebook
Ouachita Trail guidebook
Arkansas Wildflowers guidebook (Don Kurz)
Missouri's Natural Wonders guidebook (Don Kurz)
Illinois Wildflowers guidebook (Don Kurz)

**Find these guidebooks in your local bookstore, outdoor store,
or park visitor center; or online at www.UAPress.com.**
For more info contact us at:
<u>www.TimErnst.com</u>

To my mother, Eva Wheeler, for teaching me early on to appreciate nature and all that God has given us. And for letting me know there is nothing you can't accomplish if you set your mind to it.

To my Dad, Wib Wheeler, who was a great man and, in his passing, taught me more about life than most have taught me while living.

To my wife, Stacey, for believing in me and supporting me when others were telling us we were nuts and that we would never make it, or that your husband should just give up and get a real job.

And to my kids, Elizabeth and Zane, for sharing many swimming holes, trails and magical moments with me. You two knuckleheads have given me more than you will ever know.

I thank God for letting me know each and every one of you!

"The Old Swimming Hole"

Old swimming holes where our grandparents played,
still hold the magic for their grandkids today.

With the passing of time, bathing suits have changed.
But the fun and frolic remain the same.

Grandpa went swimming in his overalls,
now grandson's suit is tight and small.
Grandma pinned her long dress between her legs,
now granddaughter's suit is only string and lace.

A cold biscuit and ham was a picnic in the past,
carried to the swimming hole in a brown paper bag.

Now a cooler of ice packed with bologna and cheese
can be found in the back of a new SUV

The boys still woo the girls with their high dives.
The girls still giggle and flutter their eyes.

Times have changed but the water still flows.
Friends still find magic at the old swimming hole.

Eva Wheeler

Table of Contents

Introduction

Few things compare to the thrill of an actual swimmin' hole in the summertime. The purpose of this book is to help you, the reader, find and enjoy a few of the best ones to be found in the Ozarks of northern Arkansas and southern Missouri.

From the beginning, I set forth some standards that each swimming hole had to meet to make the book. First of all, each one had to be on public property or private with established public access. Each one had to be reachable by vehicle or on foot. If on foot, the hike had to be two miles or less, one way. Most holes had to be at least six feet deep in average conditions and have something to offer besides just being wet. Some of the featured swimming holes were exempted from the six-foot rule due to an extraordinary amount of uniqueness or great value for something such as being kid friendly and safe.

All of the swimming holes featured in this book are on streams of some sort, whether it be a river, creek or spring, or on small lakes. I did not include any large lake/impoundment locations because that is a different subject. And I'm sure many local favorites were left out; for each one I've listed, there are dozens more.

I also left out a great many swimming holes on creeks and rivers that have to be reached by boat. The Buffalo River, for instance, has great swimming holes literally around almost every bend. There are many great books that feature Arkansas' larger streams and include such information.

I have tried to be as accurate as possible on distances and directions and fees at the time I visited. I have also tried to make the directions as simple and easy to understand as possible. I have personally been to each of the swimming holes listed (please don't feel sorry for me, someone had to do it) so that I could ensure the accuracy of the information.

In the following pages, I will touch on safety, tips to help you better enjoy your visit and each visitor's responsibility so that every subsequent visitor can enjoy their trip as well. Who knows, I may even add a few of my own thoughts along the way. Please remember that some of these are in wild places and most have no lifeguard. They are all fun to visit, but be careful, you are doing so at your own risk (take another look at the warning on page one!).

Please, enjoy the book and use it as often as you can. But more importantly, enjoy the featured areas as much and as often as you can and introduce someone new to the joy of the swimming hole, especially a kid!

SAFETY! FIRST AND FOREMOST

Before we even begin the drive or hike to the first swimming hole, we must discuss the issue of safety. After all, visiting swimming holes in wild places is much different than a trip to the city pool. When you take it upon yourself to go to these places, you do so at your own risk. There are no lifeguards or first aid stations and medical assistance can literally be hours away. But, barring an unavoidable accident, if you just use a little common sense the rewards usually far outweigh the dangers.

Skills:

As with most activities, safety begins at home. It seems obvious, but do you know how to swim? Are you confident enough in your ability to get yourself, or someone else, out of a bad situation? If not, stick to less "adventurous" swimming until you feel your abilities are sufficient.

First Aid:

Know at least some basic first aid and CPR so you can help if someone gets hurt, or direct someone if you do. There generally is no reason to pack in a first aid kit designed for a rain forest expedition, but maybe a little gauze to help control bleeding or a CPR mask in case of the worst. A modern snakebite kit called "The Extractor" is also a handy item, but more about snakes and snakebites later.

Planning:

Let someone know where you are going and when you plan on getting back. If you're not back within a reasonable time frame, those looking for you at least have a place to start. Also, having someone along with you not only makes the trip more enjoyable, but if something happens, one of you may be able to go for help.

Lost?:

What if you get lost? First of all, if you feel like you may be lost, stop and sit down. Relax for a minute and try to evaluate the situation. If you still feel you may be lost, admit it. Trying to save a little pride and continuing to wander aimlessly can quickly put your situation in a downhill slide. If you truly are lost, the most important thing you can do is stay put, and don't panic. Let me repeat that one, ahem—STAY PUT AND DON'T PANIC!!!!!!! Even on a day hike, getting turned around or a little off course can be fatal if you panic. But if you stay calm and remain where you are, chances are that you will come out of it just fine.

Let's be realistic about the situation for a minute. First of all, you are in the Ozarks, and even though there is some big and wild country left in both Arkansas and Missouri, you are not in the vast wilderness of Alaska. I am not trying to downplay Ozark wilderness, as you can get just as lost and just as dead here as anywhere. All I'm saying is that if you stay put and do what you should, you'll probably be celebrating your rescue over a steak in a day or so. Secondly, the original purpose of your trip was to go swimming, so it probably isn't the middle of January. You probably aren't going to freeze to death.

On the other hand, if you go wandering around the woods trying to "fix" the situation, several things are going on. First of all, you are very possibly walking away from anywhere searchers are going to be coming from. If you are up moving around, you won't be able to hear the searchers calling your name. You are also using up all your energy and are dehydrating at the same time (it's summertime, find a shady spot and let them come to you!).

Walking around in the woods, especially as it starts to get dark, adds other dangers as well. You are much more likely to be bitten by a snake, or fall off a bluff. It's hard to fall off a bluff sitting against a tree and a snake is not likely to approach and bite you.

Animals:

Speaking of snakes, there are a few venomous snakes in the Ozarks. And one of the most aggressive, the cottonmouth or water moccasin, lives in close proximity to the water. Most snakebites occur because the snake feels threatened. A snake is not likely to go out of its way to bite you; in fact it will usually avoid you in any way possible. But if you step on him or poke a stick at him, then he is going to feel obligated to bite you. The best policy with snakes is to just avoid them and watch your step. If you are not sure if a snake is venomous, leave it alone.

Earlier I mentioned snakebite extractors. If you are close to help, these are not usually recommended as they can be damaging. Besides, a vast majority of venomous snakebites are "dry bites" meaning little or no venom is injected into the victim. If you are an hour or more from help, the extractor might be necessary. If you or a member of your party is bitten and it is believed venom was injected, decide where the nearest medical assistance is located. If you are not comfortable with trying to get the victim to help first, use the extractor as directed. It could mean the difference between an uncomfortable ride and a purely miserable one. I should note that in the United States very few snakebites are fatal. Many are, however, extremely painful, cause intense swelling and splitting open of the skin and bring illness unlike most folks have ever experienced. I have heard snakebite victims say that during the worst part, they had actually wished they were dead.

I should take a moment to mention bears. Bears were reintroduced to the Ozarks years ago and are now doing well. Chances are very slim, however, that you will ever encounter one in the wild. You may be in close proximity to them on several occasions, but probably will never know it. Bears, like most wild animals, will generally avoid contact with humans.

Injured bears and mothers with young are about the only bears that pose much threat to humans. If you should stumble onto one or more bear cubs, pay close attention looking for momma and vacate the premises. If you happen upon an injured bear, once again leave immediately and report it to the agency in charge of the particular area you are in (such as National Park Service, Arkansas State Parks, etc.), a local game and fish or wildlive officer, or local law enforcement.

Jumping/Diving:

Another concern when swimming in nature is underwater objects such as rocks or logs. Many swimming holes are popular due to jumping off rocks or swings. These make the place much more fun, but care should be taken to ensure that the activity is safe. Just because you jumped off the same rock last month doesn't necessarily mean it's safe today. If some type of object has washed downstream since the last time you were here, it may be tragic. Check the safety of the hole before jumping in. Several fatalities or crippling injuries occur each year from jumping or diving accidents (please read warning on page one!).

Water Conditions:

Swimmers also need to take the water conditions into account. Unlike the local pool, streams can hide some pretty intense currents. All of the swimming holes listed in this book are normally safe, but they can all also become death traps with a little rain. If the water is muddy and running big, then you definitely should not attempt to swim in it. This is another place you will need to use some common sense. If the water is moving too fast, stay out of it!! Moving water is considered to be one of nature's strongest forces. One foot of moving water can easily wash a full-sized pickup downstream if the conditions are right. No matter how strong your swimming abilities, you are no match for that.

On the other hand, what if it hasn't rained in a month and there is little water in the swimming hole? If the water appears stagnant, avoid it too. Some nasty little bugs can live in stagnant water, especially if animals have been using it to drink, cool off and everything else animals do in water during the heat of the summer.

Each year we can't wait to start doing the fun stuff we haven't gotten to do since last summer, but trying to swim when it is still too cold can also be very dangerous. Don't push the envelope on starting too early in the year or trying to keep swimming too late in the season.

Hypothermia can set in at a very rapid rate in water; in fact the body loses heat in the water about 30 times faster than in the air. "Immersion" hypothermia is, just as the name implies, caused by immersion in water. Cold water can overwhelm the body's ability to respond to the hostile environment it has just been plunged into. The body's normal defense is to immediately reduce the circulation to the "shell areas." These are the extremities and the surface areas. This in turn allows more blood to the core of the body in an attempt to keep the organs alive. The body also begins to try to produce heat by burning stored fuel and by inducing exercise (shivering is a form of involuntary exercise).

Generally in our climate, hypothermia is not life threatening except in the coldest months. It can lead to other problems though. Early signs of hypothermia are shivering, being uncoordinated, and mild to moderate changes in mental status. Hypothermia is famous for decreasing judgment. It is very easy to get lost on the hike out with a mild to moderate case of hypothermia, due to the judgment factor. Another danger is in the aforementioned case of decreased blood flow to the extremities. With decreased blood flow comes decreased ability to use the extremities. This can often lead to drowning, sometimes even before the signs of hypothermia are recognized.

One final note on immersion hypothermia—the water does not have to be ice-cold to induce the problem. In fact, even in tropical waters, hypothermia can slowly begin to set in without you knowing. Think of it like this—any water that is lower in temperature than your body will begin to drain the body of heat. The farther below the body temperature the water is, the faster this drain occurs.

Sun Exposure:

The sun is a great and wonderful big ball of fire in the sky. It cheers us up, keeps the earth alive and is key in growing our potatoes for the tater chips you pack in to the swimming hole. The sun can also be dangerous. Take the necessary precautions against sun damage such as the long-term stuff like skin cancer and the short-term stuff like severe sunburn.

A mild or moderate sunburn can be very uncomfortable, but a severe one can be downright dangerous. Several years ago, I was floating the Buffalo River early in the summer. My bare, neon white legs were left unprotected and exposed to hours of direct sunlight. The result, as you might imagine, was a severe burn that resulted in actual water blisters and an infection and inflammation of my shinbones. It warranted a trip to the local emergency room, antibiotics and missed work. It could have even been much worse. Some simple precautions such as a waterproof sun block or protective clothing can go a long way in preventing you from having such experiences. Pay especially close attention to the kids and keep their sensitive skin covered.

As I mentioned earlier, a little common sense goes a long way. Just pay attention to the conditions and be ready to react should an incident occur. Take a basic first aid course, including CPR, and stay calm. If you have kids along, watch them extra close. Be SAFE and have FUN!!

RESPONSIBILITY

All of the swimming holes listed in this book are treasures and we all should be able to enjoy them. But with that privilege comes a responsibility: a responsibility to the environment, to other users and to yourself.

Keep It Clean:

We all have to take care of nature. This can start with something as simple as not littering or polluting. Don't leave trash behind, and if some slob before you has done so, pick it up and bring it out with you.

Don't put things in the water that will pollute it. No one wants to be downstream from some type of funky pollutant, and as you have probably been told, we're all downstream.

Don't bring glass containers. Glass is easily broken and can become an immediate as well as long-term hazard to you and other swimmers. In fact, many state and national parks do not allow glass containers on streams. If there is something you just have to have on the trip and it is in a glass jar or bottle, transfer it to something else. A gaping, bleeding gash on the bottom of a foot can spell real trouble when there is a two-mile hike back to the vehicle.

Etiquette:

When you are in these lovely areas, be respectful of others. While it is just fine to have a great time, yelling and so forth, others may be seeking quiet and tranquility. Some may be reading or reflecting. Some great swimming holes are great fishing holes too. This isn't to say you can't do your thing, just give them some room as well.

Watch your language when in the presence of others, especially if they have children along. And be aware of your attire, or lack thereof. Some places seem to have been made for skinny-dipping, however going nude is illegal in most places, so be sure to check your local regulations before getting that all-over tan.

Protect It:

This kind of follows the "keep it clean" part. If you build a fire (check local rules and regulations), keep it under control and make sure it is *completely* out before leaving it. If it does get out of hand, report it immediately. The sooner it is reported the better the chances of containing it. Don't feel that you are better off not reporting it. If you allowed the fire to get out of control, you may be subject to fines. But most folks don't know that you can also be ordered to repay such things as the costs of manpower, equipment, fuel, and whatever is required to put out the fire. In addition, you may have to fork over some major bucks for things such as the value of the damaged timber or structures that became engulfed. I would much rather pay a ticket for being honest than to be indebted for years for trying to avoid the responsibility. And in a vast majority of the cases, officials are able to determine who was responsible for the blaze.

Don't drive in areas not designated for vehicles. While it can be great fun and perfectly fine to take your four-wheel drive or ATV off road, some areas are very sensitive and prone to damage such as erosion or harm to rare plant life or animal habitat.

Share It:

Share these special places with others. The more people that grow to love a place, the more voices there are for its preservation. By taking children to these places and teaching them to love and care for them, we are introducing a whole new generation of conservationists. As the rally cry for many conservation issues goes, "Pass it on"!

Support Nature:

There are many wonderful organizations out there that are dedicated to nature in one way or another. Pick a few that you agree with and feel will do the most good and support them with your time and money. Small donations go a long way if we all pitch in. Most people don't realize (or admit) that a majority of nature conservation money comes from sportsmen (and women) buying hunting or fishing licenses or outdoor equipment. Even if you don't fish or hunt, purchasing a license can go a long ways toward the care of our environment.

Volunteering is another good way to help out. Whether it is out in the woods doing stream or trail maintenance, helping with local bird counts or wildlife assistance programs, or teaching local children about nature and why WE need to protect it, a few hours here and there can mean many years of positive impact.

These natural areas have seen little change in many eons of "progress" and it is our responsibility to keep it that way. So enjoy them but care for them too.

Thank Yous

This book would not have been possible without the help of a lot of folks. To each of you I owe a great deal of gratitude and thanks. Many of you helped in so many ways and if I don't mention any particular deed, you know what you contributed.

First of all, I want to thank God for not only letting me do this, but for making all these places for me to write about in the first place.

Thanks go out to my wife Stacey for coming up with the idea, helping with all the work and putting up with me through all of this. Stacey, thank you also for giving me the two best earthly gifts of my life, our daughter, Elizabeth and our son, Zane. Both of whom, I hope to spend many hours in the swimming hole with.

Thanks to my mother, Eva Wheeler, for teaching me to appreciate nature and life in all their glory. And to my late father, Wib Wheeler, for teaching me so much about the reality of life so early.

Thanks to Jesse Scribner for tagging along, helping out and putting up with me on a road trip or two and for helping me obey the road signs. Jesse also shot a few pictures for the book, and endured frigid waters to model for the cover shot.

Thank you to Tim Ernst for first inspiring me years ago to take the best pictures and write the best prose I could (both of which still need a lot of work). Then for continuing to inspire, support and guide me until this day and playing a huge role in this book, including publishing it. And to Pam Ernst for keeping me going with the little race we had. (No thanks to you for kicking my butt, though.) I can't wait until next time, you had better get ready!!

Thanks to all the tourism professionals who gave me information about their area and put me in touch with the right folks and found places for me to stay at night. Tourism professionals in general are a good lot and will go out of their way to help anyone needing information about their area. Special tourism thanks goes out to Susan Wade with the Springfield, Missouri Convention and Visitors Bureau, Andy Thiem with the Pulaski County, Missouri Tourism Bureau, Carol Zeman and Joel Pottinger with the Lake of the Ozarks Convention and Visitors Bureau, and Jim Zaleski of the Joplin Convention and Visitors Bureau.

Thanks to all the individuals who called or e-mailed me with good information, told me about swimming holes in conversation, or helped out in some other way—especially Greg and Judy Harris, David Eastep, Terry and LeBeta Yeager,

Jason Crader, Don Kurz, Andy Ostmeyer with the *Joplin Globe,* Wayne Backler with the *Springfield Newsleader*, Fred Pfister with *The Ozarks Mountaineer,* Carol Biermann, Bill Bens, Tari Underwood, Alicia Usery (one of our cover models), Larry D. Degraff, G.D. Sanders, Rita Martin, Allen and Karen Armer, Jim Trammell, Don Stanley, Cindy Prince, Alisa Scribner, John Moore, Lynn Still, Kerry Saterfield, Dennis Middleton, Tina Smith, Laura Marshall with the National Park Service at Buffalo Point, Jodi Towery with the National Park Service at Big Spring, Audra Phillips with the Forest Service in Paris, Arkansas, James Dicknell with the Forest Service. Not all of the swimming holes made the book (but maybe in round two), but I really did appreciate the information and the help.

And definitely, thanks to you for taking the time to read this book, I sincerely hope you are able to get out and enjoy as many of these special places as possible. Just remember to stay safe, care for these places and please introduce a kid to them.

Make A Splash!!!

Glenn W. Wheeler

Kicking back at the "Tie Slide" overlook, upriver from Tyler Bend, on the way to the Love-Hensley Hole.

Arkansas Swimming Holes
(not on the Buffalo River)

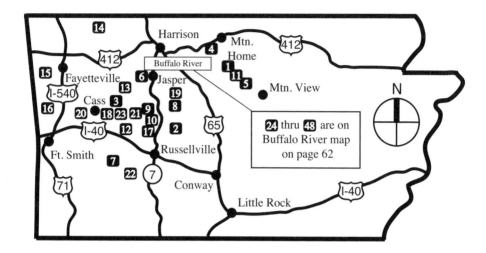

All of the swimming holes included in this section are the ones in the Arkansas Ozarks that are not along the Buffalo River. Most are in the Ozark National Forest. Two are actually south of the Arkansas River and not even in the Ozarks, but are within the boundaries of the Ozark National Forest and are so neat that I just had to include them (Spring Lake and Cove Lake—you will love them both). What great fun it was to see many parts of Arkansas I don't get to spend much time in!

For more information about the Ozark National Forest go to:
www.fs.fed.us/oonf/ozark/

#16 Lee Creek, Highway 220 Bridge

Lee Creek, Crawford County, Arkansas

Agency: U.S. Forest Service, Ozark National Forest
Nearby community or landmark: Devil's Den State Park, Van Buren, Arkansas
GPS: N: 35°42'12" W: 94°19'38"
Access: Vehicle
Day Use Fee: None
Facilities: None
Activities: • primitive camping • swimming • fishing
Alerts: None

This is a great hole of water that is easy to get to. The downstream end is shallow enough for the little guys to play in, but upstream is a great jumping off rock that you can actually drive out on top of.

The rock is actually a small bluff with a six or eight foot drop to the deep, cool water. There are no facilities here, but folks occasionally camp in the large parking area.

If you are visiting Devil's Den State Park (where they only allow swimming in the pool), come south on Highway 220 (this section is still dirt) for 8.2 miles. Just after the road turns to pavement, you will cross a bridge spanning Lee Creek. Just past the end of the bridge, you will see a turnoff to the left. Turn here and you will see the parking area just ahead.

You can also look at your Arkansas map and find the intersection of Highways 59 and 220 (just north of Cedarville). From that intersection, take Highway 220 north for 9.4 miles and turn right just before crossing the bridge.

Some folks regularly drive up from the Fort Smith area to enjoy this little jewel. It can sometimes get a little busy, but doesn't seem to get overly crowded.

Emergency: Crawford County Sheriff, 479–471–3260

Lee Creek, Highway 220 Bridge

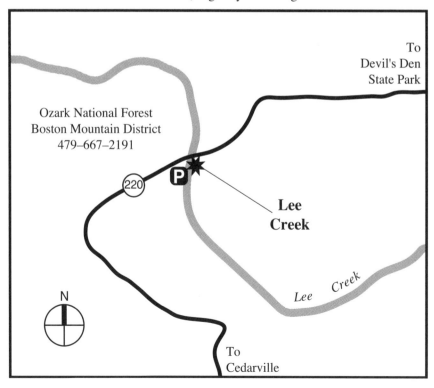

To
Devil's Den
State Park

Ozark National Forest
Boston Mountain District
479–667–2191

220

Lee
Creek

Lee Creek

N

To
Cedarville

#15 Lake Wedington

Lake Wedington, Washington County, Arkansas

Agency: U.S. Forest Service, Ozark National Forest
Nearby community or landmark: Fayetteville, Arkansas
GPS: N: 36°05'20" W: 94°22'22"
Access: Vehicle
Day Use Fee: Yes
Facilities: • campsites • comfort stations with flushing facilities • sinks • showers • trails • snack bar • lodge • playground • swimming area • pay phone
Activities: • swimming • hiking • fishing • canoeing • camping
Alerts: None

Lake Wedington is an old campground on a small lake just west of Fayetteville, Arkansas. Many of the buildings on the property were built by the CCC around the time of the great depression and still have a lot of charm. The day use portion of the park is clean and well-kept. The camping area is not maintained but is still a good place to pitch a tent. All the campsites are basic with a picnic table, fire grate and lantern pole.

From Interstate 540 in Fayetteville, exit onto Highway 16 west. Travel west 12.2 miles, to the second Lake Wedington entrance (the first one is the campground). Turn left across from the large brown sign and proceed to the gate shack. They will either take your use fees there, or post a sign directing you to the snack bar. After passing the gate shack, take the first left into the large parking area. You will see the lakeside snack bar building and the roped-off swimming area is directly in front of it.

This little place is very handy if you are in the Fayetteville area. It can however, get a little busy and is not as secluded as others. It is definitely worth a trip out here though, especially with the kids.

Emergency: Washington County Sheriff, 479–444–1850

Lake Wedington

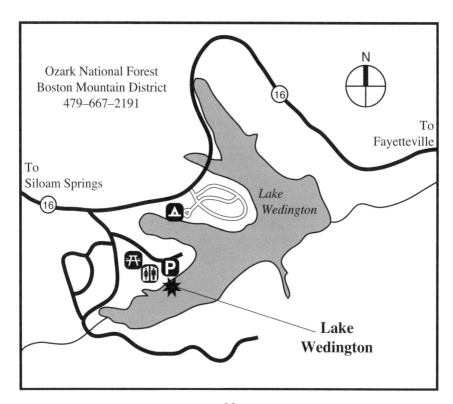

Ozark National Forest
Boston Mountain District
479–667–2191

N

To
Fayetteville

To
Siloam Springs

16

16

*Lake
Wedington*

**Lake
Wedington**

#14 Lake Leatherwood

Lake Leatherwood, Carroll County, Arkansas

Agency: City of Eureka Springs, Arkansas
Nearby community or landmark: Eureka Springs, Arkansas
GPS: N: 36°26'04" W: 93°45'32"
Access: Vehicle
Day Use Fee: Yes
Facilities: • swimming area • dive platform • camping • cabins • hiking and biking trails • boat ramp and dock • playground • visitor center • bath house • drinking water • baseball and soccer fields • pay phone
Activities: • swimming • fishing • boating (no wake) • camping • lodging • playing • hiking • biking
Alerts: None

Lake Leatherwood is a very neat, 85-acre lake within a 1600-acre city park that is owned by the City of Eureka Springs, Arkansas. There are small cottage type cabins available to rent and camping in the park. There is a bathhouse, running water, and a boat ramp and dock. There is even a rock diving platform that was built by the WPA.

The city has over 15 miles of hiking and biking trails within the park as well as baseball and soccer fields and playgrounds for the kids. Not to mention you are just minutes outside one of the most unique towns in the nation.

From the intersection of Highways 23 and 62 in Eureka Springs, go west on Highway 62 for 3.2 miles (go left at the "T" at 0.4 mile, still Highway 62). At 3.2 miles, turn right onto Carroll County Road 204 at the large "Lake Leatherwood" sign. Follow that for 1.4 miles to the parking area. Park near the large bathhouse; the swimming hole and dive platform are behind it and down the hill.

You can learn more about it at **www.cityofeurekasprings.org**.

Emergency: Eureka Springs Police, 479–253–8666

Lake Leatherwood

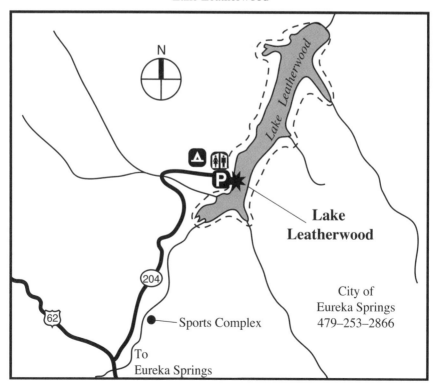

Lake Leatherwood

City of
Eureka Springs
479–253–2866

Sports Complex

204

62

To
Eureka Springs

#20 Shores Lake
Shores Lake, Franklin County, Arkansas

Agency: U.S. Forest Service, Ozark National Forest
Nearby community or landmark: Fern, Arkansas
GPS: N35°38'25" W93°57'35"
Access: Vehicle
Day Use Fee: Yes
Facilities: • campground with either primitive sites or sites with electric hook up • group pavilion • water • both chemical toilets and flushing toilets with showers • pay phone • swimming area • hiking trails • boat launch • picnic areas • handicap facilities
Activities: • swimming • fishing • hiking • camping • picnicking • boating • hunting in the area
Alerts: None

Shores Lake Recreation Area is a wonderful place, located in the Ozark National Forest, near White Rock Mountain. White Rock Mountain is a great place to take in some of the best views to be found in the south end of the Ozarks. But be careful, especially with kids and pets; the trails run right along the rim of some pretty impressive bluffs. One wrong step and you could quickly become a statistic! If you make it to Shores Lake, I suggest you drive (or hike) up to White Rock.

The Shores Lake area itself is nestled in a beautiful valley not far from the Mulberry River. The campground and recreation area are very nice, well-kept and quiet. Shores Lake is an 82-acre impoundment that is as clear and scenic as a small lake in the mountains should be. The swimming area is a roped-off area on the north end of the lake and has nearby changing shelters, bathrooms, tables, benches and a group pavilion. Also nearby is a small boat launch area, but boats are not allowed in the swimming area.

To reach Shores Lake from Interstate 40, take Highway 215 (Mulberry Exit 24) north for 12 miles (through the community of Fern) to Bliss Ridge Road/Forest Road 1505 (paved), where you will turn left. Follow Bliss Ridge Road for 1 mile and turn right at the sign, and follow that to the parking area just ahead. (Bliss Ridge Road continues on past the campground, turns to gravel, and eventually connects to the roads that go up to White Rock Mountain).

You can also get to Shores Lake from Highway 23 near Cass, but it is mostly gravel road. Begin at the Turner Bend store next to the Mulberry River (supplies, canoes, and camping, plus great hospitality, local information and terrific sandwiches), then head north on Highway 23 and turn left onto Shores Lake Road (gravel). Follow it 10 miles, where it will turn into paved Highway 215 (nice overlook at 9.6 miles—the view down to Shores Lake is incredible!). Continue another 1.7 miles and turn right onto Bliss Ridge Road (Forest Road 1505). Follow Bliss Ridge Road for 1 mile and turn right and follow that to the parking area.

Emergency: Franklin County Sheriff, 479–667–4127

Shores Lake

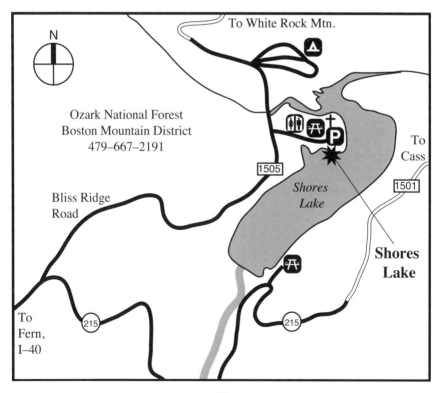

N

To White Rock Mtn.

Ozark National Forest
Boston Mountain District
479–667–2191

1505

Bliss Ridge
Road

*Shores
Lake*

To
Cass

1501

**Shores
Lake**

To
Fern,
I–40

215

215

#18 Redding Campground
Mulberry River, Franklin County, Arkansas

Agency: U.S. Forest Service, Ozark National Forest
Nearby community or landmark: Cass, Arkansas
GPS: N35°40'55" W93°47'13"
Access: Vehicle
Day Use Fee: Yes
Facilities: • campground • toilets • showers • drinking water • canoe access • hiking trails
Activities: • swimming • fishing • canoeing • hiking • hunting in the area
Alerts: None

Redding is a campground and canoe access on the Mulberry Wild and Scenic River. The Ozark Highlands Trail also passes nearby and the Spy Rock Loop Trail located here connects with it.

To reach Redding from Interstate 40, go north on Highway 23 (Exit 35) for 13.7 miles to Cass, Arkansas. Just north of the CCC work station, turn right onto Highway 215. Follow Highway 215 for 2.7 miles and turn right onto Forest Road 1003-N. Follow Forest Road 1003-N for 0.7 mile to the parking area. Don't forget to stop at the pay station for your fees. The swimming hole is visible from the parking area.

Emergency: Franklin County Sheriff, 479–667–4127

Redding Campground, Mulberry River

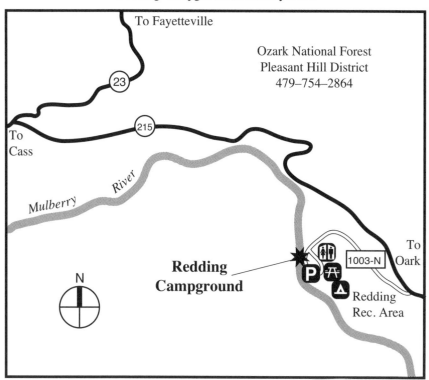

#23 Wolf Pen Campground
Mulberry River, Johnson County, Arkansas

Agency: U.S. Forest Service, Ozark National Forest
Nearby community or landmark: Cass, Arkansas
GPS: N 35°40'32" W 93°37'49"
Access: Vehicle
Day Use Fee: Yes
Facilities: • picnic tables • toilets • campground
Activities: • swimming • fishing • canoeing • camping
Alerts: None

Wolf Pen is another one of the access points for the Mulberry Wild and Scenic River and has a nice swimming hole and picnic area. It is a little more secluded than Redding, but is worth the drive if Redding is crowded. The drive is also very scenic and the Yale Church (11.3 miles from Highway 23) is definitely worth a look.

To find Wolf Pen from Interstate 40, go north on Highway 23 (Exit 35) for 13.7 miles to Cass, Arkansas. Just north of the CCC work station, turn right onto Highway 215. Follow Highway 215 for 12.5 miles (some of it may be gravel, but will eventually all be paved). At 12.5 miles, turn right onto Forest Road 1003-L and follow that 0.1 mile to the parking area next to the pay station.

From the parking area, follow the trail that runs down the steps and over to the picnic area. The swimming hole is just below the picnic tables.

Emergency: Johnson County Sheriff, 479–754–2200

Wolf Pen Campground, Mulberry River

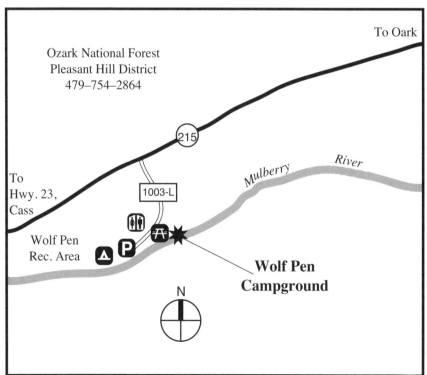

Ozark National Forest
Pleasant Hill District
479–754–2864

To Oark

215

Mulberry River

To
Hwy. 23,
Cass

1003-L

Wolf Pen
Rec. Area

**Wolf Pen
Campground**

N

#12 Horsehead Lake

Horsehead Lake, Johnson County, Arkansas

Agency: U.S. Forest Service, Ozark National Forest
Nearby community or landmark: Harmony, Arkansas
GPS: N 35°33'52" W 93°38'23"
Access: Vehicle
Day Use Fee: Yes
Facilities: • campground • bathrooms with showers • changing shelter • swimming area • boat launch • playground • drinking water • pay phone
Activities: • swimming • fishing • camping • boating • picnicking • playing
Alerts: None

Horsehead Lake is a Forest Service recreational area and an Arkansas Game and Fish Commission fishing lake. A couple of years ago a tornado struck the area and devastated the campground and some beautiful old trees that grew there. The campground has since undergone extensive renovations and is a super place to visit.

The swimming area is a roped-off section of the clean, clear-water lake and the water is regularly tested for quality, making this a great place to take the kids. There are nice bathrooms by the lake with changing facilities, flushing toilets and showers. Despite the designated swimming area, there is no lifeguard on duty. This little lake is definitely worth the trip.

To find Horsehead Lake from the intersection of Highways 64 and 103 in Clarksville, go north on Highway 103 for 8.4 miles and turn left onto Highway 164. Follow Highway 164 for 3.5 miles to Forest Road 1408C. Follow Forest Road 1408C for 2.2 miles (staying on the pavement) to the parking area near the playground.

The swimming hole is visible from the parking area.

Emergency: Johnson County Sheriff, 479–754–2200

Horsehead Lake

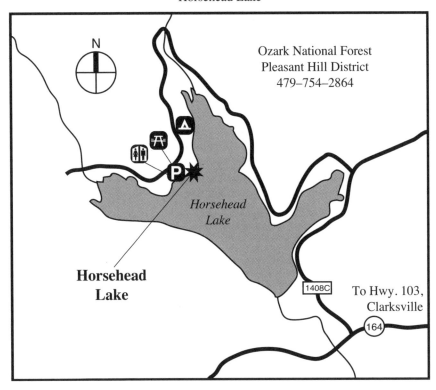

Ozark National Forest
Pleasant Hill District
479–754–2864

Horsehead Lake

Horsehead Lake

1408C

To Hwy. 103,
Clarksville

164

#3 Big Hole (aka Blue Hole)
Little Mulberry Creek, Madison County, Arkansas

Agency: U.S. Forest Service, Ozark National Forest
Nearby community or landmark: Boston, Arkansas
GPS: N: 35°48'16" W: 93°33'22"
Access: Four-wheel drive or high clearance vehicle
Day Use Fee: None
Facilities: None
Activities: • swimming • fishing
Alerts: Somewhat remote, road can get difficult, rocks can get slick, check for hazards before jumping/swinging, help is a LONG ways away.

Yep, this is another Blue Hole, but this is a real jewel; a top-notch swimming hole that is pretty out-of-the-way but definitely worth the trip. The road down to the swimming hole can get pretty difficult to do after a good rain, high clearance is always needed and four-wheel drive will be called for at times.

The swimming hole itself is pretty big and deep for this little creek and is very scenic to boot. There are some good boulders in the pool and there is sometimes a rope swing. The hole of water is fed by a cascading waterfall/slide and is surrounded on three sides by rock ledges. Just upstream are some neat little waterfalls. You will pass them on the way in. This one has apparently even been published as the best skinny-dipping hole in Madison County. I visited it in March after a big rain. It was damp and cold and the water was up, so I can't vouch for the skinny-dipping part.

To find this hidden treasure from the junction of Highways 16 and 21 in Fallsville, Arkansas, go west on Highway 16 for 14.8 miles and turn left onto Madison County Road 4258 (Forest Road 1459). If you are coming from the west, the road is 1.3 miles east of the community of Boston. Reset your trip meter here.

Once turning off the highway, the road will immediately "Y," then take the left. At 0.3 mile it looks as if you are on a driveway, but keep going, it will pass the house you see. Take the right at 1.2 miles and the left at 2.0 miles. Just keep following the road until it dead ends at 3.5 miles (as the road comes to Little Mulberry Creek, turn right and go downstream—do not cross the creek). Park there and the swimming hole is just to your left.

Emergency: Madison County Sheriff, 479–738–2320

Big Hole, Little Mulberry Creek

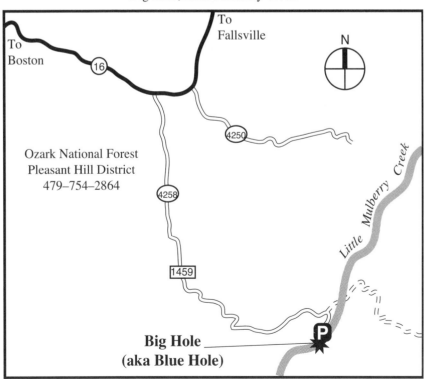

#13 Kings River Falls
Kings River, Madison County, Arkansas

Agency: Arkansas Natural Heritage Commission
Nearby community or landmark: Boston, Arkansas
GPS: N: 35°54'11" W: 93°34'47"
Access: Short, easy hike (1.2 miles roundtrip)
Day Use Fee: None
Facilities: None
Activities: • swimming • hiking • fishing • waterfall hunting
Alerts: There is private property at the trailhead—be respectful.

Kings River Falls is a great place for a lot of activities. It is a wonderful, short trail for a family or group hike. The trail is perfect for wildflowers in season, has some historical interest, and some terrific waterfalls. Next to the main waterfall and swimming hole, the rocks are a nice place for a picnic or a nap. We have led several kids' group hikes to this spot and the kids (including me) splashed for hours! I highly recommend this one, and Elizabeth and Zane do as well.

To reach Kings River Falls, grab your map and find Boston. It is in Madison County, between Red Star and Pettigrew on Highway 16. Boston was once a thriving community and there are still several buildings around. Once in Boston, go north from Highway 16 on County Road 3175 for 2.0 miles to the fork. Go right at the fork (County Road 3415) and continue for 2.3 miles to the "T" intersection. At the "T," turn left onto County Road 3500; within a few yards you will cross a creek—the parking area is on the right at the big Arkansas Natural Area sign next to a hayfield.

From the parking area, the trail to the swimming hole goes past the sign and runs next to the hayfield, following a small creek. Soon the trail comes to a metal footbridge crossing another small creek, then turns right. The trail then follows alongside Kings River downstream. You will pass a century-old, hand-built rock fence that is a true testament to the blood, sweat and tears early Ozarkers put into the land they loved.

Not far past the rock fence you will come to the Natural Heritage Commission's sign—you are almost there! Just a short distance more and a small creek crossing and you are at the waterfall. The total distance to the waterfall is 0.6 mile, one way.

The waterfall spills into a really nice pool that has good water most of the year. Once you have checked the hole for depth and hidden debris, the rocks make a good platform from which to do your best redneck water jumps. Just don't forget to yell, "hey y'all, watch this!"

www.naturalheritage.com/
Emergency: Madison County Sheriff, 479–738–2320

Kings River Falls, Kings River

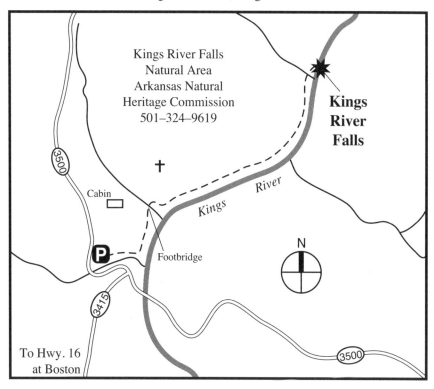

Kings River Falls
Natural Area
Arkansas Natural
Heritage Commission
501–324–9619

Kings River Falls

3500

Cabin

River

Kings

P

Footbridge

N

3415

To Hwy. 16
at Boston

3500

#21 Slot Rock

Lick Creek, Johnson County, Arkansas

Agency: U.S. Forest Service, Ozark National Forest
Nearby community or landmark: Ozone, Arkansas
GPS: N: 35°40'56" W: 93°21'79"
Access: 2.2-mile hike on Ozark Highlands Trail (4.4 miles round trip), or a short hike after a rough trip in a four-wheel drive vehicle
Day Use Fee: None
Facilities: None
Activities: • swimming • hiking • hunting
Alerts: Remote, seasonal

Slot Rock is a neat waterfall and swimming hole along the Ozark Highlands Trail. If you are hiking this stretch of the trail and the water is good, this is a great cooling-off spot. The hike is part of Section Five in Tim Ernst's *Ozark Highlands Trail Guidebook.*

If you are just coming to check out the swimming hole, here are the directions: From the community of Ozone, Arkansas, go north on Highway 21 for 6.7 miles and turn right onto County Road 5570/Forest Road 1003, which later becomes County Road 5680. OR from Fallsville, Arkansas, go south on Highway 21 for 7.2 miles and turn left onto County Road 5570/Forest Road 1003.

Once on County Road 5570/Forest Road 1003, go 6.9 miles to County Road 5671/Forest Road1004 and turn right. Go 5.1 miles and park where the Ozark Highlands Trail crosses the road. OR if you are at Haw Creek Campground, go south on Highway 123 for 3.3 miles and turn right onto County Road 5741/Forest Road 1003 (becomes County Road 5680), and go about 7.7 miles and turn left on County Road 5671/Forest Road 1004. Go 5.1 miles and park where the OHT crosses the road.

(It is also possible to get to this area by driving on down the hill from the OHT trailhead area and turning right onto County Road 5550/Forest Road 1405, and then crossing Lick Creek, following it upstream towards the swimming hole—see the map at right. The last part of this road is *very* rough and requires a serious four-wheel drive vehicle; then you will still have to park and hike—if you can find a spot to park in the woods.)

From the trailhead parking area on County Road 5671/Forest Road 1004, get on the OHT and head west. Follow the trail around the hillside and all the way down to where it intersects with a jeep road (this is 2.0 miles from the trailhead). The trail continues going straight across the road, but you need to turn right on the road and go about 0.2 mile where you will see Slot Rock below you on the left.

If you are coming from Fallsville, don't forget to stop at Marcia's Fallsville Store at the intersection and try one of those sandwiches.

Emergency: Johnson County Sheriff, 501–754–2200

Slot Rock, Lick Creek

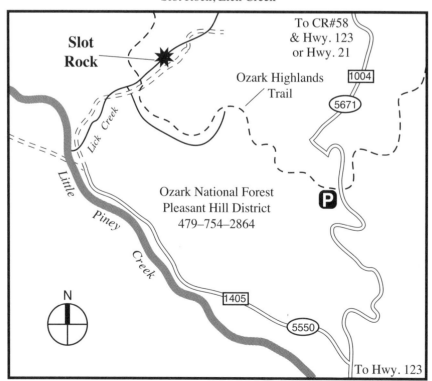

#9 Fort Douglas, Highway 123
Big Piney Creek, Johnson County, Arkansas

Agency: U.S. Forest Service, Ozark National Forest
Nearby community or landmark: Pelsor (or Sand Gap), Arkansas
GPS: N35°40'37" W: 93°14'06"
Access: Vehicle
Day Use Fee: None
Facilities: None
Activities: • swimming • hiking • canoeing • hunting • fishing
Alerts: Don't jump from the bridge.

The Fort Douglas swimming hole is located at the bridge where Highway 123 crosses Big Piney Creek. It is in the Ozark National Forest and is near Haw Creek Falls Campground.

To reach the swimming hole from Sand Gap (called Pelsor on some maps— intersection of Highways 7 and 123), go west on Highway 123 for 11.1 miles to the bridge. Cross the bridge and turn right. You will see the parking area just down the hill. (There is a main trailhead for the Ozark Highlands Trail another 200 yards on down the highway on the left, which is next to the old Fort Douglas schoolhouse.)

If you are wanting to stay in the area, Haw Creek Falls campground is just 1.5 miles west of the bridge. If water levels are good, there are also some great waterfalls just up the road. Pam's Grotto is a beautiful stop to visit; it has a 37-foot waterfall that is very unique. Haw Creek Falls is a small waterfall, but is located right next to the campground. And just about a quarter mile from the campground is Pack Rat Falls, a nice, moss covered 24-foot falls. Check out Tim Ernst's *Arkansas Waterfalls Guidebook* for more details.

Emergency: Johnson County Sheriff, 501–754–2200

Fort Douglas, Big Piney Creek

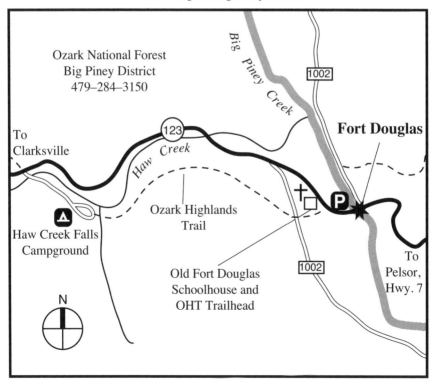

Ozark National Forest
Big Piney District
479–284–3150

Big Piney Creek

1002

Fort Douglas

To
Clarksville

123

Haw Creek

Ozark Highlands
Trail

Haw Creek Falls
Campground

Old Fort Douglas
Schoolhouse and
OHT Trailhead

1002

To
Pelsor,
Hwy. 7

N

#17 Longpool Campground

Big Piney Creek, Pope County, Arkansas

Agency: U.S. Forest Service, Ozark National Forest
Nearby community or landmark: Dover, Arkansas
GPS: N: 35°33'00" W: 93°09'44"
Access: Vehicle
Day Use Fee: Yes
Facilities: • campground • picnic area • showers • changing stations • drinking water • running water restrooms • pay phone
Activities: • swimming • canoeing • camping • hiking • fishing • hunting • waterfall viewing
Alerts: None

Longpool is a wonderful campground and recreation area on Big Piney Creek. It is a well-maintained place with plenty of shady campsites, nice bathrooms and picnic areas. There is also a great waterfall just up the "holler" and some great swimming here.

The area is one of the main canoe access points for Big Piney Creek, so it can get crowded on certain weekends, or if there is good water. There is also a small day use fee, but it is nominal and the benefits are well worth it.

To reach Longpool from Dover, Arkansas, go north on Highway 7 to Highway 164, where you will turn left and then a quick right onto County Road 14 (old Highway 7) at the sign. The road will turn into County Road 15; follow it 4.8 miles to the recreation area. Park in the day use parking area near the bathrooms. The river is just below you.

Be sure and stop in at Moore Outdoors on the way in (back near the Highway 164 turnoff). They have a lot of good information on the area, plus canoe rentals, cold drinks, supplies you may need, and friendly folks (**www.mooreoutdoors.com**).

Emergency: Pope County Sheriff, 479–968–2558

Longpool Campground, Big Piney Creek

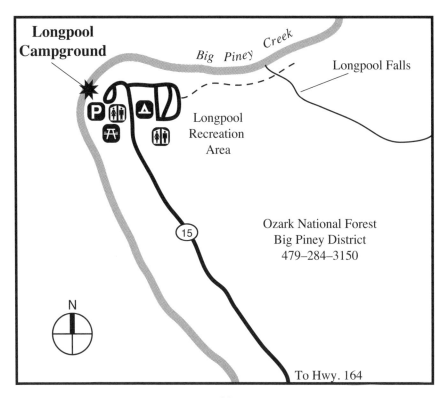

Longpool Campground

Big Piney Creek

Longpool Falls

Longpool Recreation Area

Ozark National Forest
Big Piney District
479–284–3150

15

N

To Hwy. 164

#10 Mouth of Graves Creek
Big Piney Creek, Pope County, Arkansas

Agency: U.S. Forest Service, Ozark National Forest
Nearby community or landmark: Dover, Arkansas
GPS: N: 35°35'10" W: 93°10'20"
Access: Good four-wheel drive, ATV, horseback or foot
Day Use Fee: None
Facilities: None
Activities: • swimming • fishing • canoeing • primitive camping • hunting • ATV riding
Alerts: Remote, road can get pretty rough.

This hole is located on a bend in Big Piney Creek just below where Graves Creek runs into it. There is a decent-sized opening for primitive camping, but getting there can be pretty rough. A GOOD four-wheel drive is needed and if the creeks are up a little, I wouldn't try it. The last little section of road before the parking area is the worst and it might pay off in the long run to park a little ways up the hill and walk the rest of the way in. There is one particular rock in the road that could cause some major problems. It would be a great place to ride your ATV, horse or mule to, or a pretty good hike.

To reach it from Dover, Arkansas, go north on Highway 7 for 5.4 miles and turn left onto Highway 164. Follow Highway 164 past the sign for Longpool, then across the Big Piney Creek. After crossing the bridge, turn right on County Road 16/Pilot Knob Road and go 4.5 miles. At 4.5 miles, turn right onto Forest Road 1800A and reset your trip meter here. If you don't have four-wheel drive, you will need to park at 1.6 miles and hike the rest of the way; if you do, keep going. At 3.8 miles, after you have crossed Graves Creek and made your way up the hill, take a right at the "Y." For most rigs, even four-wheel drives, it might be easiest to park here and walk the last 0.2 mile down the hill to the opening. There is a large rock in the road that creates a drop-off that may make your vehicle a long-time part of the landscape without the right equipment to get it out, and it's a LONG way to anyone from here!

Emergency: Pope County Sheriff, 479–968–2558

Mouth of Graves Creek, Big Piney Creek

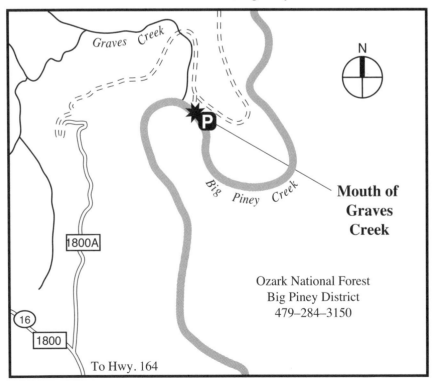

#2 Bayou Bluff

Illinois Bayou, Pope County, Arkansas

Agency: U.S. Forest Service, Ozark National Forest
Nearby community or landmark: Hector, Arkansas
GPS: N: 35°31'26" W: 92°56'33"
Access: Vehicle
Day Use Fee: None
Facilities: • campground • picnic areas and shelters • pavilion • toilets
• drinking water • hiking trail
Activities: • swimming • fishing • canoeing • camping • picnicking • hiking
• seasonal whitewater
Alerts: Be careful of the current.

Bayou Bluff is a Forest Service recreation area and campground on the Illinois Bayou north of Hector, Arkansas. This area is best known for its seasonal whitewater and can be a hot spot for kayakers, canoers and other whitewater enthusiasts when conditions are right.

From Hector, Arkansas, go north on Highway 27 for 5.5 miles to the entrance to the recreation area and park there. The swimming hole is just below you at the small bluffs. The current can get tricky sometimes, so keep that in mind.

Emergency: Pope County Sheriff, 479–968–2558

Bayou Bluff, Illinois Bayou

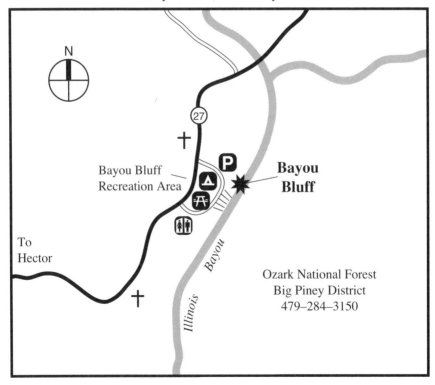

N

27

Bayou Bluff
Recreation Area

P

**Bayou
Bluff**

To
Hector

Illinois Bayou

Ozark National Forest
Big Piney District
479–284–3150

#8 Falling Water Falls

Falling Water Creek, Pope County, Arkansas

Agency: U.S. Forest Service, Ozark National Forest
Nearby community or landmark: Ben Hur, Arkansas
GPS: N: 35°43'19" W: 92°56'58"
Access: Vehicle
Day Use Fee: None
Facilities: None
Activities: • swimming • kayaking • fishing
Alerts: Rocks can be slick; check for water depth and underwater hazards before jumping off bluff or using rope swing.

Falling Water Falls is a great little waterfall (about ten feet tall) that spills into a nice hole of water that is perfect for jumping into or swinging into from the rope swing above. Just be careful when jumping or swinging, make sure the water is deep enough and that no debris has washed in underwater.

This is also a famous local kayaking spot when the water is up. Folks like to ride their boats over the falls, which is a sight to see.

To reach Falling Water Falls, from Pelsor (called Sand Gap on some maps), go east on Highway 16 through the community of Ben Hur for 9.8 miles from Highway 7 to Forest Road 1205/County Road 68 and turn left. Go 2.3 miles and park along the road in the new parking area right next to the creek. The creek will be to your right.

Another seven miles down the road (continuing as you were going) is Richland Creek Campground, where there is another great swimming hole (see the following pages).

Emergency: Pope County Sheriff, 479–968–2558

Falling Water Falls, Falling Water Creek

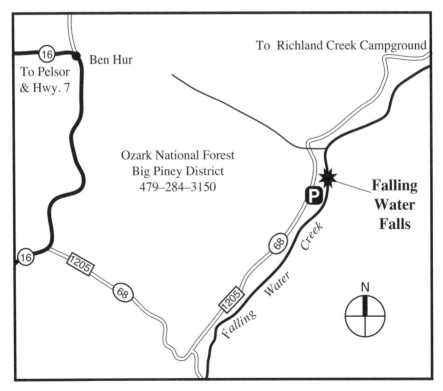

To Richland Creek Campground

16
Ben Hur
To Pelsor
& Hwy. 7

Ozark National Forest
Big Piney District
479–284–3150

Falling
Water
Falls

P

68

16
1205
68

1205

Falling Water Creek

N

#19 Richland Creek Campground
Richland Creek, Searcy County, Arkansas

Agency: U.S. Forest Service, Ozark National Forest
Nearby community or landmark: Ben Hur, Arkansas
GPS: N: 35°47'51" W: 92°55'56"
Access: Vehicle
Day Use Fee: None
Facilities: • basic campsites • hiking trails
Activities: • swimming • hiking • camping • fishing • hunting
Alerts: Somewhat remote

If you are looking for a superb swimming hole that is both out-of-the-way and not a major undertaking to get to, this is one of the top spots in Arkansas. You can drive to a small campground by the swimming hole that is maintained by the U.S. Forest Service, but it is not heavily used. Park or camp here and the swimming hole is just below you. This particular hole has some gorgeous boulders in the upstream end and a bluff across the creek.

Richland Creek is one of the most scenic small streams in the area. After swimming in the main hole, slip your shoes on and start upstream. There are several more fantastic swimming holes within easy walking distance that provide more privacy and solitude.

Some of the best hiking in the area can be found nearby. The little hike up to The Twin Falls of Devil's Fork would be a great side trip. There are also some wonderful waterfalls nearby when the water level is up.

One of the nearby waterfalls is Falling Water Falls, which also has another one of the best swimming holes around (see the previous page). Also check out Six Finger Falls, which is also very close by. Drive just minutes up the main road, park in the pull-off and walk about 15 yards to a very unusual and scenic spot. Check out Tim Ernst's ***Arkansas Waterfalls Guidebook*** for great information on these waterfalls and many more.

To find Richland Creek Campground, take Highway 7 to Pelsor, Arkansas (also known as Sand Gap on some maps). It is between Jasper and Russellville, Arkansas, near the Newton/Pope County line. There you will find one intersection and one store. Go east on Highway 16 for 9.8 miles to County Road 68. Follow County Road 68 (staying left) for 9.4 miles to the campground. Pull into the campground, and follow the road to the creek. The swimming hole will be on your right.

Emergency: Searcy County Sheriff, 870–448–2340

Richland Creek Campground, Richland Creek

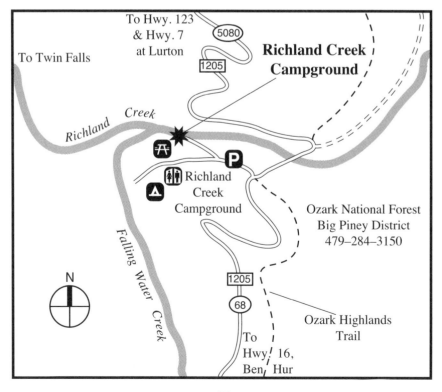

To Hwy. 123 & Hwy. 7 at Lurton

5080

1205

To Twin Falls

Richland Creek Campground

Creek

Richland

Richland Creek Campground

Ozark National Forest
Big Piney District
479–284–3150

N

Falling Water Creek

1205

68

To Hwy. 16, Ben Hur

Ozark Highlands Trail

#6 Bradley Park

Little Buffalo River, Newton County, Arkansas

Agency: City of Jasper
Nearby community or landmark: Inside City of Jasper, Arkansas
GPS: N: 36°00'31" W: 93°11'25"
Access: Vehicle
Day Use Fee: None
Facilities: • basketball courts • baseball field • pavilion • picnicking • playground • walking trail
Activities: • swimming • fishing
Alerts: None

This is a neat combination. There is a really good swimming hole at the City Park in Jasper, Arkansas. Jasper is a small town (population 489), with a lot of small town charm. There is some great lodging in the area and terrific restaurants. If you're hungry, try Point of View on Highway 74 west, The Ozark Café or The Dairy Diner on Highway 7 in Jasper. Or drive a few miles south of town on Highway 7 to The Cliff House for not only a great meal, but one of the best views to be had at any restaurant.

The park is nice and well-kept, with few frills. The swimming hole is in the Little Buffalo River, which flows into the famous Buffalo National River a few miles downstream.

Since this is a city park, the swimming hole can sometimes get a little busy. Not to worry though, it is a long hole of water that actually goes around a bend in the river. Even if several folks are there, you should still have plenty of elbow room.

From Harrison, go south on Highway 7 for 16.4 miles to the town of Jasper. Continue into Jasper until you come to a 90-degree curve to the left. After the curve (you are still on Highway 7) take the second right which is Clark Street. Go 0.4 mile on Clark Street (past the school) to the entrance of Bradley Park.

Once in the park, stay to the right at the first intersection. Continue to the next intersection and turn right again. There is a small gravel parking area almost immediately to your left, before the pavilion. If the parking area is full you can park along the road. The swimming hole is just a few yards down the hill.

A neat side stop is the Bradley House Museum, which is also on Clark Street (you will pass it on the way in). The Bradley House is run by the Newton County Historical Society and has some great displays of pioneer life in the area. There is even a reconstructed, late 1800's cabin out back. They also sell some of the best books about Newton County, and the Ozarks in general.

FYI, there is a spot called "Little Bluff" a little ways upstream from Bradley Park where the locals go for some serious bluff-jumping—tall bluff, deep pool below. The area is on private property and so not included in this guidebook.

Emergency: Newton County Sheriff, 870–446–5124

Bradley Park, Little Buffalo River

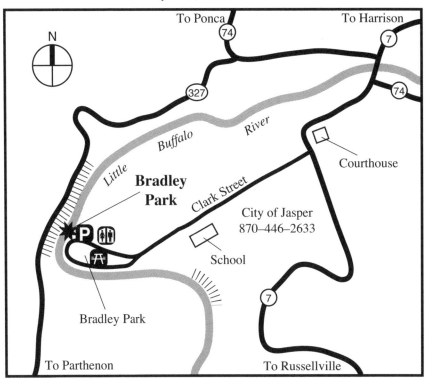

#4 Big Spring, Cotter
Big Spring, Baxter County, Arkansas

Agency: City of Cotter
Nearby community or landmark: Cotter, Arkansas
GPS: N: 36°15'58" W: 92°32'35"
Access: Vehicle
Day Use Fee: None
Facilities: • city park with pavilion • picnic area • restrooms with running water • swing for the swimming hole • baseball field • playground • boat launch • railroad memorial • privately owned trout dock next door • pay phone
Activities: • swimming • fishing • playing • picnicking • boating
Alerts: COLD WATER!! The trout dock is privately owned and the owners have it clearly posted. Respect their rights and don't park on their lot.

Big Spring is just that, a big spring located in a city park in Cotter, Arkansas. And since it is a spring, the water is COLD! There is a permanent steel beam there for a rope swing to swing out into the water. As you swing out and are about to reach the peak of your pendulum and unwrap your fingers from the rope, just remember........I told you it was cold!!

Cotter is located between Harrison and Mountain Home on Highway 62/412. The directions given are coming from the Harrison area. From the intersection of Highways 65 and 62/412 just south of Harrison, go east on Highway 62/412 for 34.9 miles. At the top of the hill after you have crossed the bridge spanning the White River, you will turn right (south) onto Highway 62-B in Cotter. Reset your trip meter here. Follow Highway 62-B through town, and at 1.8 miles it will make a 90-degree turn to the right towards the old historic bridge—you will want to stay straight at this corner and not go toward the bridge. Go another 0.1 mile and take the next right and follow that road on down to the gravel parking area. The swimming hole is right next to it.

Emergency: Baxter County Sheriff, 870–425–6222

Big Spring at Cotter

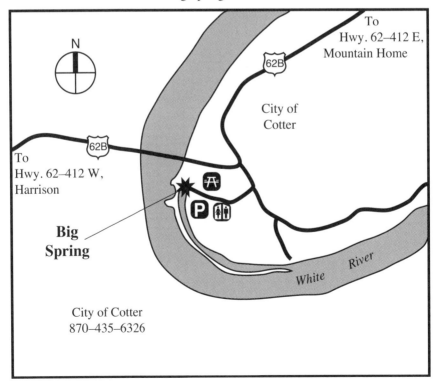

N

To
Hwy. 62–412 E,
Mountain Home

62B

City of
Cotter

62B

To
Hwy. 62–412 W,
Harrison

**Big
Spring**

P

White River

City of Cotter
870–435–6326

#1 Barkshed Campground
North Sylamore Creek, Stone County, Arkansas

Agency: U.S. Forest Service, Ozark National Forest
Nearby community or landmark: Fifty Six, Arkansas
GPS: N: 36°01'09" W: 92°15'03"
Access: Vehicle
Day Use Fee: Yes
Facilities: • picnic area • fire pits • grills • toilets • hiking trail
Activities: • primitive camping • swimming • fishing • hiking • picnicking
Alerts: Don't jump from the bridge.

Barkshed Campground is a nice quiet spot that actually has two swimming holes just a few yards apart. The swimming holes are not really large, but are sure cool even in the hot, dry part of late summer. There are a couple of nice small bluffs to swim next to, and an old bridge adds a little character. (The bridge is closed at the moment, but may reopen sometime in the future.) The picnic area is shady and clean and there is another small opening on top of some large rocks that would make a great place for a quiet lunch with the one you love.

I am going to give you directions from two different places to get to this one. First from Yellville, Arkansas, go south on Highway 14 for 38.3 miles (note: at 23.2 miles, by a convenience store, Highway 14 turns left at the "Y" intersection). At 38.3 miles from Yellville, turn left on Forest Road 1112 (County Road 55). Go 3.3 miles and take a left onto Tie Ridge Road (it remains Forest Road 1112). Follow that 1.2 miles to the parking area.

From Mountain View, Arkansas, take Highway 9 north 5.3 miles to Highway 14. Turn left on Highway 14 and go 10.3 miles to Forest Road 1115 (Cartwright Road, County Road 56). Turn right and follow that to the parking area (it turns into Forest Road 1112).

Once in the parking area, the trails to the two swimming holes are obvious. There is one under and upstream of the bridge and there is one just downstream. There are also some rules here to be aware of: no pets in the water or on the gravel bars, no jumping from the rocks, no alcohol or glass on the beach, kids under eight have to be supervised, and no throwing rocks. Other than that, just have a ball!

Emergency: Stone County Sheriff, 870–269–3825

Barkshed Campground (lower hole), North Sylamore Creek

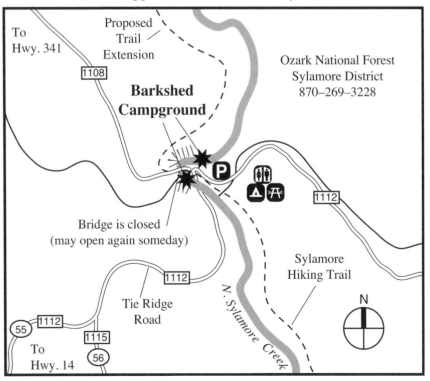

To Hwy. 341

Proposed Trail Extension

1108

Barkshed Campground

Ozark National Forest
Sylamore District
870–269–3228

P

1112

Bridge is closed
(may open again someday)

Sylamore
Hiking Trail

1112

Tie Ridge Road

N. Sylamore Creek

N

55 1112

1115

To Hwy. 14 56

#11 Gunner Pool Campground

North Sylamore Creek, Stone County, Arkansas

Agency: U.S. Forest Service, Ozark National Forest
Nearby community or landmark: Fifty Six, Arkansas
GPS: N:35°59'39" W:92°12'39"
Access: Vehicle
Day Use Fee: Yes
Facilities: • 27 campsites with grills • tables • lantern poles • tent pads (no hookups) • toilets • picnic tables • drinking water • hiking trails
Activities: • swimming • hiking • fishing • hunting • picnicking • camping
Alerts: None

Gunner Pool Campground is a U.S. Forest Service recreation area with a nice, shaded campground, picnic area, great hunting and a nice (but shallow) swimming hole. The recreation area is within the Sylamore Wildlife Management Area, which allows hunting, and the recreation area joins a "Walk-in Turkey Hunting Area." There is also an old dam on one of the tributaries that makes a nice pool for fishing, but while we were there working on the book, it had been drained. I'm not sure if the Forest Service plans to fill it back up or not.

Again, I am going to give you directions from both Yellville, Arkansas, and from Mountain View, Arkansas. From Yellville, Arkansas, go south on Highway 14 for 45.1 miles to Forest Road 1102 (Gunner Pool Road) and turn left. If you are coming from Mountain View, Arkansas, go north on Highway 9 for 5.3 miles to Highway 14 and turn left. Follow Highway 14 for 7.3 miles and turn right onto Forest Road 1102 (Gunner Pool Road).

Once on Gunner Pool Road (Forest Road 1102) go 2.7 miles to the campground. Take the last right turn, just before crossing the bridge to get to the parking area for swimming. The swimming area is just down the hill to the left. This can get pretty shallow in late summer, but is still a great cooling-off spot after a hike in the area, or the kids can play in the water while you kick back on the shaded gravel bar enjoying your weekend campout.

Emergency: Stone County Sheriff, 870–269–3825

Gunner Pool Campground, North Sylamore Creek

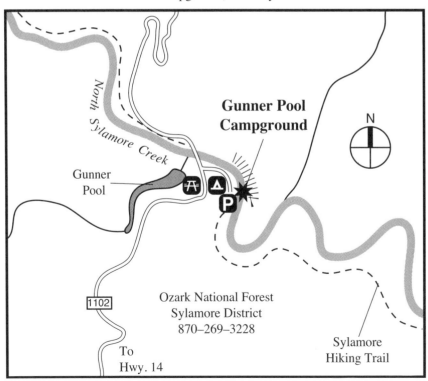

Gunner Pool Campground

North Sylamore Creek

Gunner Pool

N

Ozark National Forest
Sylamore District
870–269–3228

Sylamore
Hiking Trail

1102

To
Hwy. 14

#5 Blanchard Springs (upper & lower holes)

North Sylamore Creek, Stone County, Arkansas

Agency: U.S. Forest Service, Ozark National Forest
Nearby community or landmark: Fifty Six, Arkansas
GPS: Upper: N35°58"23" W92°10'38"
      Lower: N35°58'05" W92°10'19"
Access: Vehicle
Day Use Fee: Yes
Facilities: • visitors center • 32 campsites with grills • tables • lantern poles • tent pads (no hookups) • 2 group camps for 8 to 50 folks • dump station • restrooms with hot showers • trails • drinking water • summer interpretive tours • guided cave tours • fishing (with fish pier and handicapped access) • covered pavilion • amphitheater • pay phone
Activities: • swimming • hiking • camping • fishing • cave tours
Alerts: None

Blanchard Springs Recreation Area is a great place to spend some time. There are guided cave tours, great camping sites, a beautiful spring to visit, a wonderful visitors center with good folks working there, super hiking, fishing at Mirror Lake (complete with handicapped access and a fishing pier) and two good swimming holes. If you are looking for a top-notch place to bring the family for a getaway, Blanchard Springs is worth a look. Visitor center—888–757–2246.

As with a couple of others in this area, I am going to give you directions for coming from both Yellville, Arkansas, and Mountain View, Arkansas. From Yellville, Arkansas, go south on Highway 14 for 46 miles to the Blanchard Springs Recreation Area access road. Turn left.

From Mountain View, Arkansas, go north on Highway 9 for 5.3 miles to the intersection of Highway 14 and turn left. Go 6.4 miles and turn right at the Blanchard Springs signs, into the recreation area.

Once you have turned onto the access road from either way, the directions are the same. Continue into the park (you will come to a side road at 1.5 miles, but stay straight). At 2.4 miles you will come to a "T" intersection—turn left. After turning left you can either turn at the first right to go to the lower swimming hole, or go straight to the upper swimming hole. The lower swimming hole is just below the parking lot. The upper one is to your right, just after crossing a low water slab. Pick up a map at the visitors center to find all the other goodies Blanchard Springs has to offer.

There are also some nice swimming holes upstream that would make for a nice adventure to wander up the trail and find your favorite.

Emergency: Stone County Sheriff, 870–269–3825

Blanchard Springs (upper hole), North Sylamore Creek

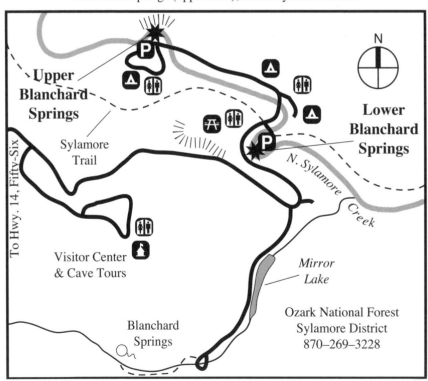

Upper
**Blanchard
Springs**

Sylamore
Trail

To Hwy. 14, Fifty-Six

Visitor Center
& Cave Tours

Blanchard
Springs

N

**Lower
Blanchard
Springs**

N. Sylamore Creek

*Mirror
Lake*

Ozark National Forest
Sylamore District
870–269–3228

#7 Cove Lake

Cove Lake, Logan County, Arkansas

Agency: U.S. Forest Service, Ozark National Forest
Nearby community or landmark: Paris, Arkansas
GPS: N: 35°13'43" W: 93°37'34"
Access: Vehicle
Day Use Fee: Yes
Facilities: • campground • picnic tables • playground • drinking water • boat ramp • marked swimming area • restrooms with hot showers • hiking trails • pavilion • seasonal food service • boat rentals • pay phone
Activities: • swimming • fishing • boating • camping • picnicking • hiking
Alerts: None

Cove Lake is one of two swimming holes in this book that are not technically in the Ozarks, but both are in the Ozark National Forest (Spring Lake is the other one), and both are very nice and worth including.

Cove Lake is a 160-acre lake near Mt. Magazine, the highest point of elevation in Arkansas, and the drive to the lake from Paris is scenic and enjoyable. There are some nice facilities including a campground, seasonal food service, and boat rentals.

From the intersection of Highways 22 and 309/109 in Paris, Arkansas, go south on Highway 309/109 for one mile until they split. Go left on Highway 309 for 7.7 miles. Just after crossing the bridge, turn left at the Cove Lake sign. Once off the highway, go left at the "Y" at 0.1 mile and continue another 0.1 mile to the parking area. The swimming area is just below you and is marked with buoys.

Emergency: Logan County Sheriff, 479–963–3271

Cove Lake

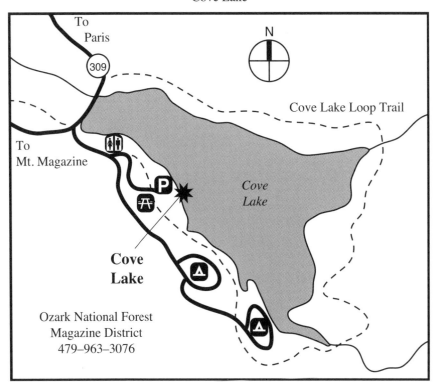

#22 Spring Lake
Spring Lake, Yell County, Arkansas

Agency: U.S. Forest Service, Ozark National Forest
Nearby community or landmark: Dardanelle, Arkansas
GPS: N: 35°09'11" W: 93°25'28"
Access: Vehicle
Day Use Fee: Yes
Facilities: • campground • marked swimming area • picnic tables • bath house with showers • drinking water • boat ramps • pavilion • pay phone
Activities: • swimming • fishing • boating • picnicking • camping
Alerts: None

Spring Lake is the other swimming hole featured (besides Cove Lake) that is not actually in the Ozarks, but is within the Ozark National Forest and is a great place to visit, so here it is.

This is one of those neat old Forest Service recreation areas and is even listed on the National Register of Historic Places. The lake is an 82-acre lake that has a marked-off swimming area.

From the intersection of Highways 22 and 27 in Dardanelle, Arkansas, go south on Highway 27 for 9.1 miles to Highway 307 and turn right (west). Take Highway 307 for 3.6 miles where it turns into Forest Road 1602. Reset your trip meter here. Follow Forest Road 1602 for 3.5 miles and turn left at the Spring Lake Recreation Area sign, onto Forest Road 1602A. Follow that 0.3 mile to the parking area by the bathhouse. The swimming hole is just below the bathouse.

Emergency: Yell County Sheriff, 479–229–4175

Spring Lake

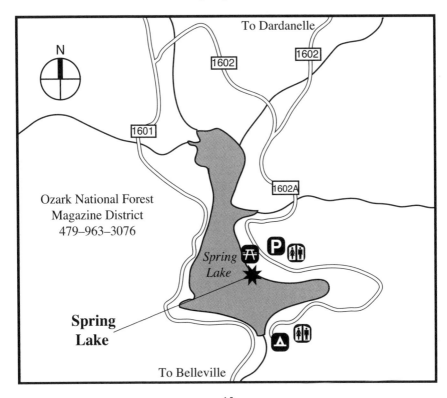

N

To Dardanelle

1602

1602

1601

1602A

Ozark National Forest
Magazine District
479–963–3076

*Spring
Lake*

**Spring
Lake**

To Belleville

Arkansas Swimming Holes
(on the Buffalo River)

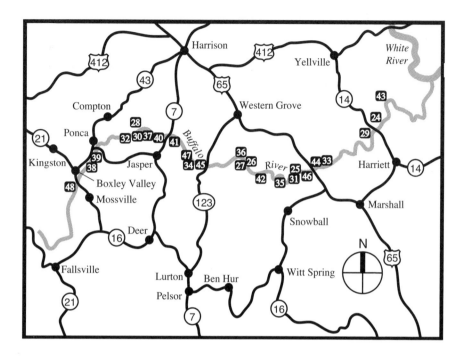

Growing up near the Buffalo River, I spent as much time on and around it as I possibly could. It has always held a special place in my heart and always will. If you have never loaded up in a canoe and spent some time on it, I recommend you do. It was made our first national river for good reason. Seems like there is a great swimming hole around just about every bend in this river, and way too many to list. Some of them will fill up with gravel one year and be too shallow, then get scoured out by flood waters the next year and be great once again. The ones listed here are some of my favorite holes that have stood the test of time. All of these holes are located within the Buffalo National River Park.

For more information about the Buffalo National River go to:
www.nps.gov/buff/

#48 Whiteley Hole
Buffalo River, Newton County, Arkansas

Agency: National Park Service, Buffalo National River
Nearby community or landmark: Boxley, Arkansas
GPS: N: 35°56'49" W: 93°24'05"
Access: Short, easy hike
Day Use Fee: None
Facilities: None
Activities: • swimming • fishing • canoeing during high water
Alerts: The hayfields are leased for farming. Respect the property.

The Whiteley family was one of the earlier families to settle in the area now known as Boxley Valley. Samuel and Lucy Whiteley, along with several children, arrived in the valley around 1835, when Arkansas was still an Indian Territory. The Whiteleys were a major part of the community for generations. This swimming hole is located on what used to be their farm and, in fact, the parking area is where one of the descendants operated a store. Part of the building stood until a couple of years ago when it was burned down. There is still a barn and other remnants of farm life there and one of the best springs around. The Whiteley Cemetery is just up the hill from Whiteley Spring.

According to "Arkansas Place Names" by Ernie Dean (*Ozarks Mountaineer*, 1986), the community was known for years as Whiteley's Mill until a merchant from Springfield, Missouri, named William Boxley moved in and the community and post office were named after him.

From the intersection of Highways 74 and 43 in Ponca, Arkansas, go south on Highway 43 for 4.2 miles to its intersection with Highway 21. Turn left (south) on Highway 21 and go 2.4 miles. Just before the highway turns left and starts uphill, there is a trailhead parking area on the right. Turn in there and park, or drive just a few yards past the parking area and park by the gate (don't block the gate or access to it).

Cross the wooden fence at the gate and follow the road/path across the field to the far side, heading toward a small bluff you can see. Once across the field, you can see where a trail starts through the woods/canebreak. Follow the trail to the river.

The swimming hole is fairly deep and has some large rocks in the middle that are good for jumping off of, although not very high. The kids love them though. There is also a nice bluff and part of the swimming hole is shaded during the day, making it a very nice place to cool off. Keep in mind that this one is far enough up the river that the water level will get low before it will farther downstream. There is usually plenty of water, but if conditions are pretty dry, you might be disappointed.

Emergency: Newton County Sheriff, 870–446–5124

Whiteley Hole, Buffalo River

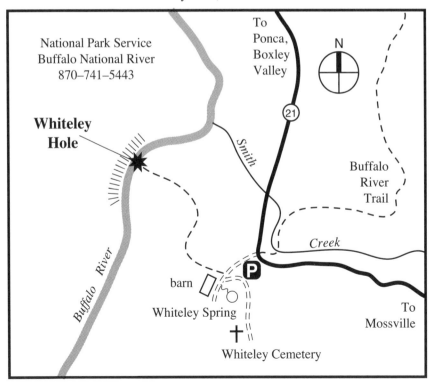

National Park Service
Buffalo National River
870–741–5443

To Ponca, Boxley Valley

N

Whiteley Hole

21

Smith

Buffalo River Trail

Buffalo River

Creek

P

barn

Whiteley Spring

To Mossville

Whiteley Cemetery

#38 Pearly Spring Hole
Buffalo River, Newton County, Arkansas

Agency: National Park Service, Buffalo National River
Nearby community or landmark: Ponca, Arkansas
GPS: N: 36°00'14" W: 93°22'12"
Access: Hike-in recommended *
Day Use Fee: None
Facilities: None
Activities: • swimming • fishing • canoeing
Alerts: We recommend that you park at the nearby scenic pulloff and hike-in.

*NOTICE: *The land on both sides of the river at this site is private property, although access to the river itself is allowed since the river and gravel bars are part of the Buffalo National River park and are public property. It is recommended that you park at the nearby scenic pulloff and hike through the gate to the river.*

This hole takes its name from Pearly Spring, which is a waterfall located across the field from this hole of water (on private property—no public access). The swimming hole is a good one, although it is just below the highway so there is some traffic noise. But after a little while here you probably won't even notice it.

From the junction of Highways 74 and 43 in Ponca, go south on Highway 43 for 1.1 miles (just past the turnoff to Lost Valley), and park at the paved scenic viewpoint on the left. Hike along the highway a short distance and turn left onto Newton County Road 8095. Follow it *steeply* down the hill through the gate to the river. If the gate was closed when you got there, be sure to close it behind you (*you are crossing private property*), both as you arrive and when you leave. The swimming hole is just upstream of the road crossing.

The nearby Lost Valley dayuse area is definitely worth the visit. If you are in this area and have some time, I highly recommend it. Maybe you could hike Lost Valley then come to the Pearly Spring Hole to cool off. The Lost Valley turnoff is 1.0 mile from the intersection of Highways 74 and 43, or 0.1 mile north of the turnoff to the swimming hole.

Emergency: Newton County Sheriff, 870–446–5124

Pearly Spring Hole, Buffalo River

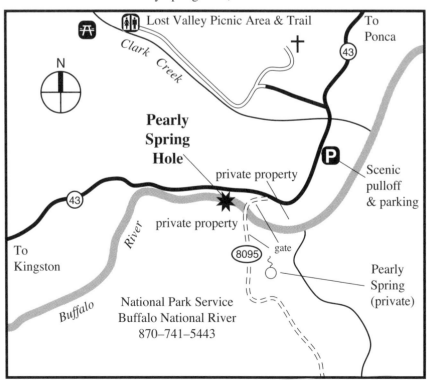

Lost Valley Picnic Area & Trail

To Ponca

Clark Creek

N

43

Pearly Spring Hole

private property

P

Scenic pulloff & parking

43

private property

To Kingston

River

8095

gate

Pearly Spring (private)

Buffalo

National Park Service
Buffalo National River
870–741–5443

#39 Ponca Low Water Bridge

Buffalo River, Newton County, Arkansas

Agency: National Park Service, Buffalo National River
Nearby community or landmark: Ponca, Arkansas
GPS: N: 36°01'16" W: 93°21'17"
Access: Vehicle
Day Use Fee: None
Facilities: • vault toilets • hiking trail
Activities: • swimming • fishing • canoeing • hiking
Alerts: If water is up much, watch the currents at the bridge.

Ponca is the uppermost access point on the Buffalo River that can be used most of the time. There is access upriver from here, but there has to be a lot of water for that stretch to be floatable. The town of Ponca is a neat little place that really took off in the early 1800's when lead and zinc mining came to town. The Ponca City Mining Company from Ponca City, Oklahoma, set up shop and it was a boomtown. There isn't any mining going on now, but some of the mines are still around. There are now plenty of canoes to rent and places to stay and be sure to check out the Elk Center in Ponca.

From the intersection of Highways 74 and 43 at Ponca, go south on Highway 43 and take the first left (about 100 yards from the intersection). Just follow the dirt road about 0.1 mile to the parking area. Most folks swim just upstream from the bridge, as it stays deep enough most of the year. If the water is up quite a bit, don't get on the upstream side of the bridge, because the currents may be too swift.

In addition to the deeper hole at the bridge, there is plenty of shallow water for the smaller ones to play in. There is some traffic noise with the new bridge just downstream and it can get pretty busy at popular canoe launch times. It can also get a little busy with swimmers from time to time as well.

If you're lucky, the elk will be in the field when you turn off the highway to drive down to the parking area. Look in the field to the right as this is one of the most common places to see the herd.

Emergency: Newton County Sheriff, 870–446–5124

Ponca Low Water Bridge, Buffalo River

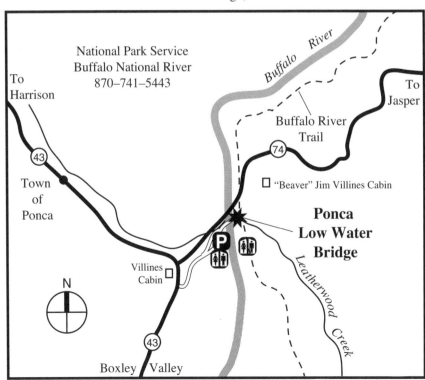

#32 Goat Bluff
Buffalo River, Newton County, Arkansas

Agency: National Park Service, Buffalo National River
Nearby community or landmark: Jasper, Arkansas
GPS: N: 36° 07' 59" W: 93° 23'26"
Access: Hike
Day Use Fee: None
Facilities: None
Activities: • swimming • fishing • hiking • canoeing • hunting
Alerts: None

Goat Bluff is a very scenic hole of water with a beautiful, tall bluff and it is just minutes away from Erbie Campground. Few folks ever go to it swimming, unless they are hiking the river trail or canoeing through.

From Harrison, Arkansas, go south on Highway 7 for 14.4 miles and turn right (west) onto Newton Counry Road 2500 (gravel) by the Erbie Access sign. Or if you are coming from Jasper, take Highway 7 north for 2 miles and turn left onto Newton Counry Road 2500.

After turning onto the dirt road, reset and go 5.9 miles and turn left into the Parker-Hickman Historical Farmstead parking area. There is a small double gate in front of you. Go through that gate (be sure and shut it behind you) and go 0.8 mile (stay left at the fork at 0.1 mile) and park beside the Cherry Grove Cemetery where the road is blocked by a cable.

Hike downhill following the old road to where the trail forks and there is a sign that says "Old River Trail" with arrows pointing each direction (this is after you have passed the Buffalo River Trail that takes off to the right also). Go right and follow the trail a couple hundred yards until you can see the river to your left. You will be at the head of a shoal there and the nice swimming is just upstream.

Emergency: Newton County Sheriff, 870–446–5124

Goat Bluff, Buffalo River

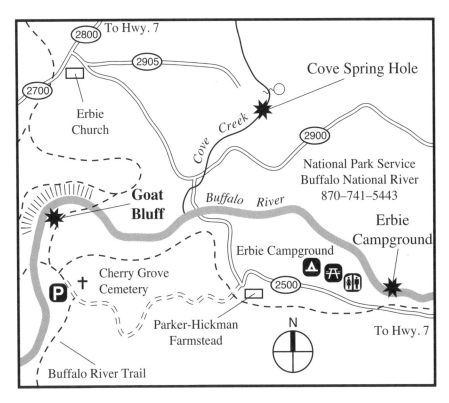

To Hwy. 7

2800

2905

2700

Erbie
Church

Cove Creek

Cove Spring Hole

2900

National Park Service
Buffalo National River
870–741–5443

**Goat
Bluff**

Buffalo River

Erbie
Campground

Cherry Grove
Cemetery

Erbie Campground

2500

P

Parker-Hickman
Farmstead

N

To Hwy. 7

Buffalo River Trail

#28 Cove Spring Hole
Cove Creek, Newton County, Arkansas

Agency: National Park Service, Buffalo National River
Nearby community or landmark: Jasper, Arkansas
GPS: N: 36°04'49" W: 93°13'16"
Access: Vehicle (sometimes four-wheel drive is needed)
Day Use Fee: None
Facilities: None
Activities: • swimming • camping • hunting
Alerts: The low water slabs on the way to this swimming hole can be extremely dangerous in high water conditions. Use your head before crossing them if the water is up.

Cove Spring Hole is a small, kind of out-of-the-way place near Erbie that is fairly easy to get to. It is on Cove Creek, which is a tributary of the Buffalo River and can be somewhat seasonal, but if the conditions are good it's great. There is a spring at the top of a small bluff along the hole that runs much of the time, spilling into the creek like a natural fountain. As I said, this swimming hole is not very big, but if there aren't already a few folks there it's worth the trip. A few of the knowledgeable locals go here when other swimming holes in the area are too crowded.

To reach it from Harrison, Arkansas, go south on Highway 7 for 14.4 miles and turn right (west) onto Newton Counry Road 2500 (gravel) by the Erbie Access sign. Or if you are coming from Jasper, take Highway 7 north for 2 miles and turn left onto Newton Counry Road 2500. Reset here and follow the road 6.3 miles to the "T" intersection. Reset and turn left toward the horse camp as indicated on the sign. Go 0.6 mile and turn right onto Newton Counry Road 2905, just before you get to the Erbie Church. Follow that road 0.7 mile to the parking area. The swimming hole is just below you.

A HUGE word of caution on this one; the low water slabs you must cross to reach this swimming hole command a lot of respect if there is much water running. In recent years several vehicles have been washed off the first one you will come to, and the river has claimed a victim or two there. There is almost always some water flowing across it, but please use caution. It doesn't take much water to wash even a full-sized pickup away. If it looks like it might be too deep, don't try it.

Alternate directions, if the Buffalo River is too high to drive across: From Hwy. 206 at Gaither, take the Erbie Cutoff Road/Newton County 2825 south (next to the water tower, paved, then gravel) for 2.2 miles then turn right onto Newton County 2800 (gravel) for 5.6 miles to Erbie; then turn left going past the church, and finally turn left onto Newton County Road 2905 to the swim hole. OR from Hwy. 7 at Marble Falls take Newton County 2800 (gravel) west 7.4 miles to Erbie; then turn left going past the church, and finally turn left onto Newton County Road 2905 to the swim hole.

Emergency: Newton County Sheriff, 870–446–5124

Cove Spring Hole, Cove Creek

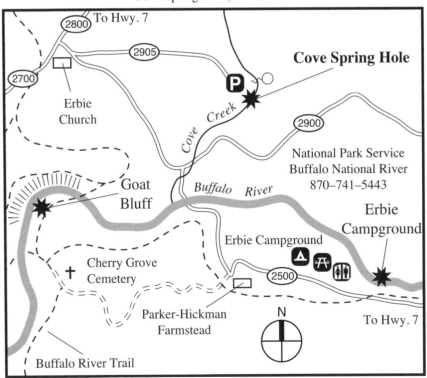

#30 Erbie Campground
Buffalo River, Newton County, Arkansas

Agency: National Park Service, Buffalo National River
Nearby community or landmark: Jasper, Arkansas
GPS: N:36°04'17" W: 93°12'44"
Access: Vehicle
Day Use Fee: None
Facilities: • campground • restrooms • drinking water • hiking/horse trails • pay phone • picnic tables
Activities: • swimming • fishing • floating • hiking • hunting • horseback riding • picnicking • historical area • wildlife watching
Alerts: Low water slab just past the campground can be extremely hazardous when the water is up.

Erbie Campground is one of several campgrounds along the Buffalo National River that is maintained by the National Park Service. There are several basic campsites with a picnic table, fire grate and a place to hang your lantern. There are no water or power hook-ups in the individual sites, but drinking water is available.

To get there go south out of Harrison, Arkansas, on Highway 7 for 14.4 miles and turn right (west) onto Newton Counry Road 2500 (gravel) by the Erbie Access sign. Or if you are coming from Jasper, take Highway 7 north for 2 miles and turn left onto Newton Counry Road 2500. Take Newton County Road 2500 5.4 miles to the campground. The Erbie area in general is a great place to see elk grazing, especially early or late in the day.

Once in the campground, take the first right. You will see a comfort station on your right and a parking area on your left. Park here and the swimming hole is right in front of you. It is easy to spot because of a gravel ramp to the water (this is also a canoe access point) and two large man-made rock formations. This hole is not extremely deep, but the surrounding area makes the visit worthwhile.

If you would like a few other activities besides swimming, there are several hiking trails (pick up Tim Ernst's *Buffalo River Hiking Trails* for some great info) and horse trails in the immediate area. Just past the campground on the main road is the Parker-Hickman Farmstead. Here you will find several buildings from years past that have been wonderfully restored and maintained.

If you continue past the Parker-Hickman Farmstead, you will soon come to a low water slab. If there is much water going over the slab, or if the water is rising—TURN AROUND, DON'T DROWN! Several people have been washed off this slab in the past few years, with at least one fatality.

After you finish swimming, you will surely have worked up an appetite. Do yourself a favor and stop at Crawford's Provisions (on Highway 7 just north of the Erbie Access road) and let Linda fix you one of her famous deli sandwiches (may I recommend "The Mountain Man" with a sarsaparilla)—you won't be sorry. Besides the deli, this is a great little store with supplies, local gifts and cabin rentals.
Emergency: Newton County Sheriff, 870–446–5124

Erbie Campground, Buffalo River

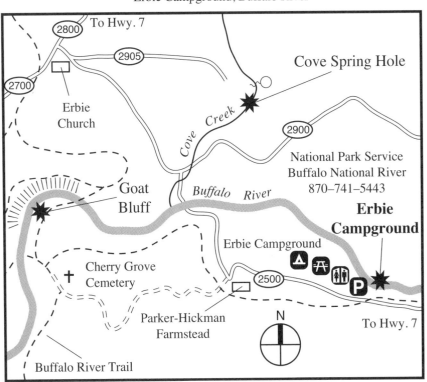

#37 Ozark Campground

Buffalo River, Newton County, Arkansas

Agency: National Park Service, Buffalo National River
Nearby community or landmark: Jasper, Arkansas
GPS: N: 36°03'54" W: 93°09'33"
Access: Vehicle
Day Use Fee: Yes
Facilities: • basic campsites • pavilion • comfort station • drinking water
• volleyball court • pay phone • small outdoor presentation area
Activities: • swimming • fishing • hiking • floating • camping • interpretive
programs
Alerts: None

Ozark Campground is a small, out-of-the-way campground on the Buffalo National River. It is usually not too crowded and is quiet and relaxing. There is a comfort station with flushing facilities, sinks and a pay phone outside. You will also find a volleyball court, a nice pavilion and a small amphitheater. In the warmer months, ranger-led interpretive programs and various presentations are common here.

The swimming hole is deeper on the lower end, but there are some interesting large rocks in the upriver end that bear checking out if you have your snorkel and mask along. There is a large gravel bar on the campground side and a large bluff on the other, making for a quiet and scenic swim.

To reach Ozark from Harrison, Arkansas, go south on Highway 7 for 13.6 miles (or 2.8 miles north on Highway 7 from Jasper) to Newton County Road 2470, the Ozark Access road. Follow the main road 1.4 miles to the campground.

The campground is laid out like a circle drive. When you enter the campground, stay right until you are opposite of the entrance. There is a large yellow sign advising of river hazards and another sign with a river map. Park here and follow the trail down the hill a few yards to the river.

For a neat side trip, you can hike to the Upper Pruitt swimming hole a little ways downriver on the Buffalo River Trail. The 2.6-mile trail starts near the entrance to the campground. It is on the right just as you come to the beginning of the "circle drive."

Emergency: Newton County Sheriff, 870–446–5124

Ozark Campground, Buffalo River

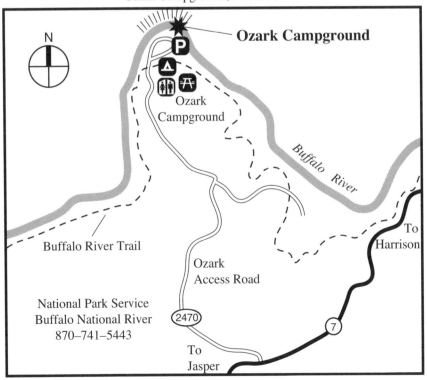

N

Ozark Campground

Ozark
Campground

Buffalo River

Buffalo River Trail

To
Harrison

Ozark
Access Road

National Park Service
Buffalo National River
870–741–5443

2470

7

To
Jasper

#40 Upper Pruitt
Buffalo River, Newton County, Arkansas

Agency: National Park Service, Buffalo National River
Nearby community or landmark: Jasper, Arkansas
GPS: N 36°03'41" W: 93°08'20"
Access: Vehicle
Day Use Fee: None
Facilities: • picnic area • toilets • pay phone
Activities: • swimming • fishing • floating • picnicking • hiking
Alerts: None

Upper Pruitt is an easy-to-reach spot with a large swimming hole and a grand bluff. The hole is deep and large enough not to feel crowded if other swimmers are around. There are a few places to jump off the bluff, but the better spot for that is the next hole down river (Lower Pruitt, see following pages).

To get there from Harrison, Arkansas, travel south on Highway 7 for 12.2 miles, then turn right just after the bridge over the Buffalo River. If you are coming from Jasper, come north on Highway 7 for 4.2 miles, then turn left just before the bridge.

Follow the trail from the parking area just a few yards to the river. You should find plenty of room on the gravel bar to sit and enjoy the view of the bluff. You will also have a view of the bridge and the traffic that uses it. For some, this is a downside, but I think the atmosphere of the place will drown out the traffic.

You may also want to hike the Buffalo River Trail 2.6 miles upriver to the Ozark Campground for another great swimming hole (see previous pages). Or you may want to drive across the bridge for the Lower Pruitt hole.

Emergency: Newton County Sheriff, 870–446–5124

Upper Pruitt, Buffalo River

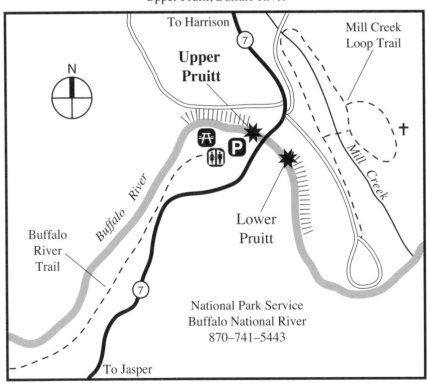

To Harrison

Mill Creek
Loop Trail

7

N

**Upper
Pruitt**

Buffalo River

Buffalo
River
Trail

Lower
Pruitt

Mill Creek

7

National Park Service
Buffalo National River
870–741–5443

To Jasper

#41 Lower Pruitt

Buffalo River, Newton County, Arkansas

Agency: National Park Service, Buffalo National River
Nearby community or landmark: Jasper, Arkansas
GPS: N: 36°03'39" W: 93°08'15"
Access: Short, easy to moderate hike
Facilities: None
Activities: • swimming • floating • fishing
Alerts: • loose footing on trail • high bluff • submerged hazards

Lower Pruitt is just downstream from Upper Pruitt. They are separated by one shoal that flows under the Pruitt Bridge. Lower Pruitt is a little harder to get to than Upper Pruitt and is not as large. It is however, just as popular, especially with local young folks.

The big draw here is the great spots to jump into the river from. There are two places on top, and several down lower. You can jump off the edge of the bluff to the green waters waiting below. Rock steps and a path have been fashioned into the bluff for an easier return trip to the top.

Use caution here though. Anytime you jump from heights like this, you are taking a risk. Underwater hazards can wash in since the last time you or someone else visited. Another hazard here is the rock cliffs themselves. After a rain or a lot of jumpers, they can become wet and slick. A really bad scenario is slipping on top of the bluff, bumping your head and falling into the waters below. Definitely don't mix alcohol or other drugs with this activity.

If you still want to brave this one, here's how you get there. From Harrison, Arkansas, go south on Highway 7 for 12 miles to the Pruitt Access road on the left (or on the right 3 miles north of Jasper). As soon as you turn off the road, park in the gravel parking area next to the big rocks.

You'll see the trail begins by going through an open area. The area sometimes gets grown up with weeds, but it is easily crossed. Follow the trail approximately 75 yards. The trail will fork; go right. Just down the hill you will come to another open area. Follow the trail to the right into the woods (watch your step, the trail usually washes out here and the footing can be a little loose) and down to the top of the bluff. Here you can jump off right in front of you or follow the trail to the left about 10 yards to another jump-off spot. If you go left, make note of the big rocks at about your 10 o'clock. If you're still up for it, take a deep breath, say a prayer and....Ger..onimo!........

Emergency: Newton County Sheriff, 870–446–5124

Lower Pruitt, Buffalo River

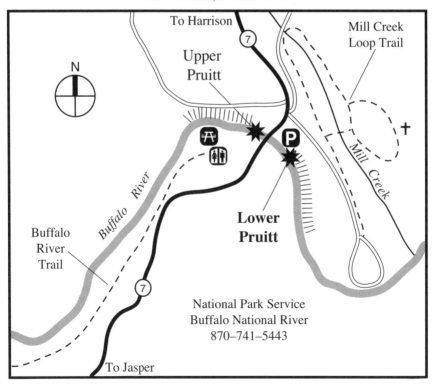

To Harrison

Mill Creek
Loop Trail

7

N

Upper
Pruitt

P

†

Mill Creek

**Lower
Pruitt**

Buffalo
River
Trail

Buffalo River

7

National Park Service
Buffalo National River
870–741–5443

To Jasper

#47 Mouth of Wells Creek

Buffalo River, Newton County, Arkansas

Agency: National Park Service, Buffalo National River
Nearby community or landmark: Hasty, Arkansas
GPS: N: 36°01'24" W: 93°06'07"
Access: Short hike
Day Use Fee: None
Facilities: None
Activities: • swimming • fishing • canoeing
Alerts: Not a very kid-friendly spot. Check for underwater hazards before jumping off the bluff. The top of the bluff can get very slick. Steer clear of private property near the parking spot.

The Mouth of Wells Creek (locally pronounced "Wells-is" Creek) is an out-of-the-way place that is popular with locals and with floaters who see it on their way by. It is a small bluff with a fairly deep hole of water below it. Be sure and go far enough down the bluff toward the downstream end to get to the deeper water. There is a small cedar tree that grows near the edge of the bluff and just past it, there is a large indention in the rock face. Along in there is where the jumping off happens. Sometimes there is even a rope or other aid there to help you climb back up. If it is not there, you really need to go to one end of the bluff or the other to get back up.

This neat little spot is near Hasty, Arkansas. To get there from the intersection of Highways 65 and 123 in Western Grove, go west on Highway 123 for 8.4 miles, just through the town of Hasty. By the Hasty Post Office, you will come to a sharp left hand curve with a dirt road that goes right. Turn right onto Netwon County Road 3800 (Gibson Dr.) and follow it. Stay straight at 0.1 mile (past road 3801) and again at 1.0 mile (past road 3802). At 1.7 miles you will come to a "Y," go left and continue 3.9 miles (old County Road 99). There you will see a small low water slab in the creek. Park in the wide spot on the left side of the road before the slab. Just across the slab is private property—be sure you're not parking or hiking there and the road is passable.

The easiest way to direct you to the swimming hole is to have you follow the creek downstream to the river. Once at the river, look to your left and you will see the end of the bluff. Make your way up the bank to the top of the bluff and follow it down to the jumping-off place described earlier.

On your way back to the vehicle, instead of going back down the bank at the upstream end of the bluff, veer off through the woods on top, keeping the creek in sight below you on your left. Parallel the creek back to the point that the level you are on makes its way back down to the creek. Once there, you are almost back to your vehicle. Just drop on down to the creek and follow it back.

As I alluded to earlier, this is probably not the place to take the little ones. Footing can be somewhat dangerous and a fall here could be tragic as help would be pretty hard to get to in a timely manner. It's also a good candidate for a "stupidity" fall when a little too much alcohol is involved. Be careful and enjoy…

Emergency: Newton County Sheriff, 870–446–5124

Mouth of Wells Creek, Buffalo River

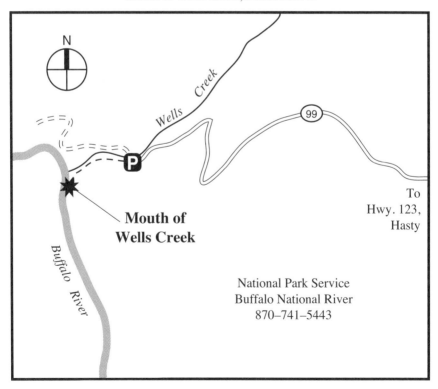

N

Wells Creek

99

P

Mouth of Wells Creek

To Hwy. 123, Hasty

Buffalo River

National Park Service
Buffalo National River
870–741–5443

#34 Hasty Campground
Buffalo River, Newton County, Arkansas

Agency: National Park Service, Buffalo National River
Nearby community or landmark: Hasty, Arkansas
GPS: N: 36°00'30" W: 93°04'53"
Access: Vehicle
Day Use Fee: None
Facilities: • toilets • two basic campsites with picnic tables • fire pits • lantern poles
Activities: • swimming • fishing • canoeing • camping
Alerts: If you venture downstream to the low water bridge, be careful of the currents. If you go up to the swing, check for hazards first.

Hasty Campground is a Park Service access point near Hasty, Arkansas. Most canoers actually take out and put in at the low water slab, but the campground and swimming access is just upstream. This is some of my old stomping grounds and I have spent many a day and night turning into a prune in this hole of water and several more within a few miles of here.

From the intersection of Highways 65 and 123 in Western Grove, Arkansas, go west on Highway 123 just after passing through Hasty, Arkansas (at 8.6 miles from Western Grove). Turn right onto Newton County Road 3850/Hasty Cutoff Road and follow it 2.5 miles to the turnoff for the campground/access, Newton County Road 3858, just past the big bridge over the Buffalo River. Follow the dirt road down the hill to the campground, about 0.1 mile.

The main swimming hole is just below you. It is a long, fairly deep hole of water with a nice gravel bar. This is a good place for several folks with kids to come to.

There is another swimming hole upstream that is pretty nice, but can be a little hit or miss. From the north end of the campground, a trail takes off through the cane and woods. Follow it until you come out on a gravel bar. Keep walking upstream until you come to the head of a long shoal. There will be a large hole of water here with a small bluff running along part of the left side. Look at the south end of the bluff and there is usually a rope swing hanging there by a high bank. It is occasionally taken down, but some of the locals usually remedy that pretty quickly and get another one back up. The bank has washed out quite a bit in the last few years, but is still usable and quite fun! Be sure and check for underwater hazards before playing Tarzan of the Buffalo, and be careful.

Emergency: Newton County Sheriff, 870–446–5124

Hasty Campground, Buffalo River

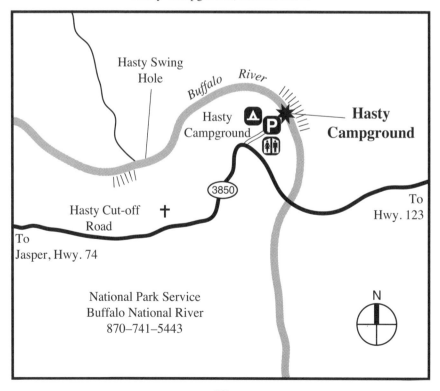

Hasty Swing Hole

Buffalo River

Hasty Campground

Hasty Campground

3850

Hasty Cut-off Road

To Jasper, Hwy. 74

To Hwy. 123

National Park Service
Buffalo National River
870–741–5443

N

#45 Troy Eddings Hole
Buffalo River, Newton County, Arkansas

Agency: National Park Service, Buffalo National River
Nearby community or landmark: Hasty, Arkansas
GPS: N: 35°58'53" W: 93°03'25"
Access: Vehicle
Day Use Fee: None
Facilities: • vault toilets • one basic campsite with picnic table • fire pit • lantern pole
Activities: • swimming • fishing • camping • canoeing
Alerts: Be careful of your footing if you check out the overlook. And, although the swimming hole and gravel bar are great for the kids, the overlook is no place for them.

The Troy Eddings Hole, also known as "The Blue Hole" (one of many), is named after an old resident of the area. It is not one of the more popular Park Service access sites, but is a great swimming and fishing hole and is popular with many locals. There is a beautiful bluff across the river, some neat rocks both out of the water and under it and a nice little creek that flows in from a shady "holler" across the way. A great gravel bar lines the other side of the hole for a long way. This is another good spot to take the family for a picnic or campout.

From the junction of Highways 65 and 123 in Western Grove, Arkansas, go west on Highway 123 for 9.9 miles. Turn right onto Newton Counry Road 3960, a small dirt road that is at the end of a white wooden fence (Blue Hole Access sign there). Reset your trip meter here and follow the dirt road 1.5 miles to the parking area. On the way in, there is an overlook with a great view at 1.0 mile—you will see the parking place on the left side of the road. Just cross the road and follow the small trail down, but REALLY watch your footing as the hillside can sometimes give way, and the first step is a killer! I wouldn't take the kids to see this overlook; it is just too dangerous.

Emergency: Newton County Sheriff, 870–446–5124

Troy Eddings Hole, Buffalo River

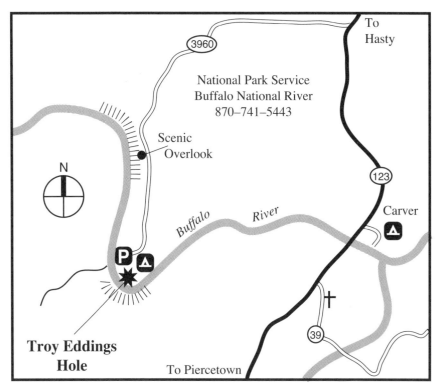

#36 Mt. Hersey
Buffalo River, Newton County, Arkansas

Agency: National Park Service, Buffalo National River
Nearby community or landmark: Pindall, Arkansas
GPS: N: 36°00'32" W: 92°57'12"
Access: Vehicle
Day Use Fee: None
Facilities: • chemical toilets
Activities: • swimming • fishing • canoeing • primitive camping
Alerts: None

Mt. Hersey is one of the National Park Service access points for the Buffalo River. Davis Creek runs into the river at the upstream end of the parking area and Mill Branch runs in just below it. There is a neat spot to visit on Mill Branch on the way in. It is an old concrete dam with a hole in it. The hole is a millrace, which once channeled the water to run a wheel for a gristmill. One day years ago as I was driving to Mt. Hersey, I looked over to see a bobcat walking across the dam. Wouldn't you know it, no camera! What a picture it would have been.

There is a pretty bluff just downstream and the upstream view is more of a tranquil view. I love it here late in the evening when the light is starting to change and all is still except for the night bugs warming up for their regular performances.

There is no deep hole of water, but it is good swimming from the parking area upstream for a ways. Davis Creek is also a good place to wade and explore. The kids can catch crawdads until they tire of it or until they can't stand the cold water any longer. It's not uncommon to see a snake or two in Davis Creek near the river, so just keep that in mind. It isn't overgrown or "snaky" as we hillbillies like to call it, so just a little care should suffice.

To reach Mt. Hersey from Western Grove, Arkansas, go south on Highway 65 for 3.8 miles (just past the turnoff to Hurricane River Cave) and turn right onto Mt. Hersey Road at the sign. Go 3.7 miles to a fork in the road—take the right fork (there is a sign indicating river access). At 1.3 miles, stay left past Newton County Road 4202). At 1.8 miles is the dam with the millrace; you can see where folks park to look at it. Keep going straight past the intersection with Newton County Road 4210 at 1.9 miles, and the parking area and river are just ahead.

Emergency: Newton County Sheriff, 870–446–5124

88

Mt. Hersey, Buffalo River

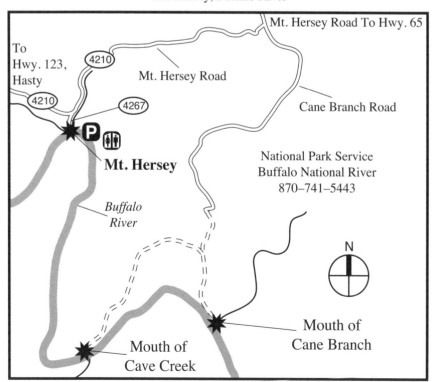

Mt. Hersey Road To Hwy. 65

To
Hwy. 123,
Hasty

4210

4210

Mt. Hersey Road

4267

Cane Branch Road

Mt. Hersey

National Park Service
Buffalo National River
870–741–5443

*Buffalo
River*

N

Mouth of
Cane Branch

Mouth of
Cave Creek

#27 Mouth of Cave Creek

Buffalo River, Newton County, Arkansas

Agency: National Park Service, Buffalo National River
Nearby community or landmark: Pindall, Arkansas
GPS: N: 35°59'03" W: 92°57'02"
Access: Four-wheel drive vehicle
Day Use Fee: None
Facilities: None
Activities: • swimming • primitive camping • fishing • hunting • canoeing
Alerts: Road can sometimes become impassable.

The Mouth of Cave Creek is one of my favorite places on this section of river to camp or fish. We like to stop here on overnight float trips and spend the night on the gravel bar, or drive in and camp, hunt or fish.

Cave Creek actually runs into the Buffalo River across from where you camp. There is a nice bluff on the creek side and a nice gravel bar on the camping side. You can also camp just up the hill from the gravel bar in an area that is not an official NPS campsite, but is open enough that it has been used for camping for years.

To reach the Mouth of Cave Creek from Western Grove, Arkansas, go south on Highway 65 for 3.8 miles (just past the turnoff to Hurricane River Cave) and turn right onto Mt. Hersey Road at the sign. Go 3.7 miles to a fork in the road—take the left fork, which is Cane Branch Road (there is a sign indicating river access on the right fork, but that is for Mt. Hersey—see previous page). Continue on Cane Branch Road for another 2.7 miles where you will turn onto the road to the right. After 0.5 mile on that road, there is another intersection—stay left and continue to the parking area at 1.7 miles.

Note: After the last intersection, the road can sometimes get pretty bad. Years ago, a friend and I thought we could get through there in a third hand Datsun B-210. Needless to say it was a LONG walk out of there, and a really big deal to get someone in there to get it out! Check the road conditions before trying that section, especially if you don't have a capable four-wheel drive. You may just want to park out on the road and take a nice hike the rest of the way in.

Emergency: Newton County Sheriff, 870–446–5124

Mouth of Cave Creek, Buffalo River

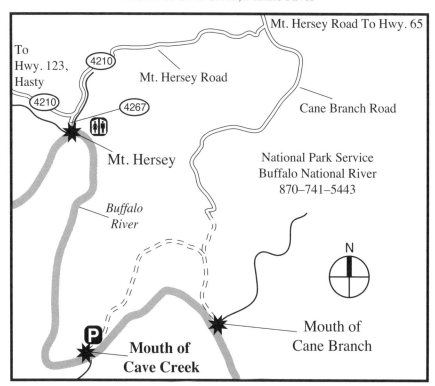

#26 Mouth of Cane Branch

Buffalo National River, Searcy County, Arkansas

Agency: National Park Service, Buffalo National River
Nearby community or landmark: Pindall, Arkansas
GPS: N: 35°59'15" W: 92°55'54"
Access: Vehicle (four-wheel drive at times)
Day Use Fee: None
Facilities: None
Activities: • swimming • canoeing • fishing • primitive camping
Alerts: None

Cane Branch flows into the Buffalo River between the access points of Mt. Hersey and Woolum. This is another place where the swimming hole is sometimes not really deep, but it is a great place to come pitch a tent and spend a couple of days. It is out-of-the-way enough to not usually draw large crowds, although it is not uncommon for families to show up.

When I was a child, some family friends would always have a family reunion there around the Fourth of July. Their ancestors had lived in the area prior to the river becoming a National Park. It was always a huge time, with a lot of the folks floating in by canoe or johnboat and the others driving in. Cane Branch has eroded its banks and has claimed part of the area where we used to camp, but there is still plenty of space left.

Where the creek flows into the river, there is usually a noticeable drop in water temperature. Downstream from the creek is usually a little deeper, but a large rock a few yards upstream can sometimes be a good spot from which to base your swimming adventures.

To reach the Mouth of Cane Branch from Western Grove, Arkansas, go south on Highway 65 for 3.8 miles (just past the turnoff to Hurricane River Cave) and turn right onto Mt. Hersey Road at the sign. Go 3.7 miles to a fork in the road—take the left fork, which is Cane Branch Road (there is a sign indicating river access on the right fork, but that is for Mt. Hersey). Go on Cane Branch Road for 3.2 miles to the parking area, right next to the river (some parts of this road near the end can be pretty rough).

Emergency: Searcy County Sheriff, 870–448–2340

Mouth of Cane Branch, Buffalo River

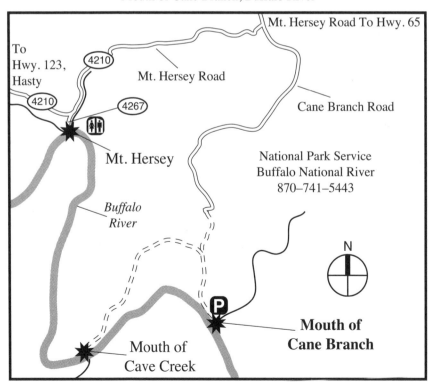

#42 Robertson Hole
Buffalo River, Searcy County, Arkansas

Agency: National Park Service, Buffalo National River
Nearby community or landmark: Pindall or St. Joe, Arkansas
GPS: N: 35°58'15" W: 92°52'46"
Access: Vehicle
Day Use Fee: None
Facilities: vault toilets
Activities: • swimming • fishing • floating • hiking • camping
Alerts: None

The Robertson Hole is just below the Woolum Access on the Buffalo River. This is a nice deep hole of water with a bluff. Sometimes there is a rope swing in the upper half of the hole, too.

Late in the summer, much of this area of the river dries up, however this hole almost never goes dry. I wouldn't recommend swimming in it in these conditions, but it is testimony to the quality of this hole of water.

There are some good camping spots to be had in the field above the river, but there are no designated camping areas. The only facilities are a couple of sets of porta-potties in the field.

To get there from St. Joe, Arkansas, take Highway 374 west. That highway will soon turn into a county road—just stay with it. At 3.6 miles you will come to a fork—stay right. Follow that road to the Woolum Access, a total of 6.7 miles.

If you are coming from the north on Highway 65, you will come to the town of Pindall, Arkansas. In Pindall, turn right on County Road 15 and follow the main road 8 miles to the "T" intersection, turn right and go 0.2 mile to the Woolum Access.

Once at Woolum, you will see a large field on your left. At the corner of that field, turn left, through the gate and follow the road 0.4 mile (just past the second set of porta-potties) to the area with the small grove of trees. You will see the bluff across the river. That's it, you're there.

A great side trip here is a bluff called the "Nars" (Narrows). It is a bluff with the river running along one side and a county road on the other. You can stand on the narrow part and look down on both. In the narrowest spot, the top of the bluff is about four feet wide. If you don't have a problem with heights, it is worth the trip.

You can only visit the Nars from here in low water conditions. To get there, go back up to the gate and turn left. You will see the gravel bar in front of you. Follow the road to the river. If the water is low enough, you can drive across at the "ford." Make sure your vehicle is up to this task; I don't recommend this in your Corvette. Once across the river (assuming you make it), drive up the bank and take a right. Follow the road around the end of the long field until it turns left. Take the left and follow it along the bluff until you see a pulloff. Park there and the trail up is visible. It's not a hard climb by any means (my daughter made it when she was about 5, although I don't recommend it for most small children), but be careful. Especially once you are on top.

Emergency: Searcy County Sheriff, 870–448–2340

Robertson Hole, Buffalo River

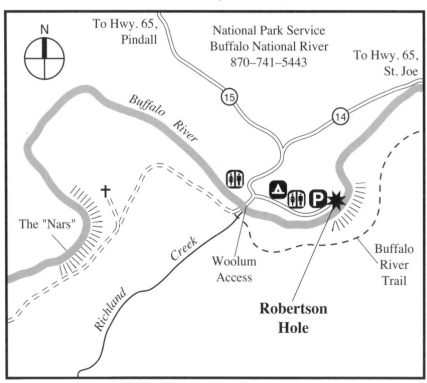

#35 Love-Hensley Hole
Buffalo River, Searcy County, Arkansas

Agency: National Park Service, Buffalo National River
Nearby community or landmark: Snowball, Arkansas
GPS: N: 35°58'01" W: 92°49'20"
Access: Four-wheel drive vehicle
Day Use Fee: None
Facilities: None
Activities: • swimming • canoeing • fishing
Alerts: None

The Love-Hensley Hole, named after a couple of local families, is a quiet, out-of-the-way place with a big, nice bluff to look at. There is a nice gravel bar and the water isn't very deep, so it would be a good place to lounge away a hot summer afternoon.

On the way to this one, you have to cross some large hay fields. Be sure and stay on the roads and don't drive out into the grass. Not only is that a good way to butt heads with someone, it is disrespectful as well.

To reach the Love-Hensley Hole from St. Joe, Arkansas, go south on Highway 65 for 5.2 miles to the Tyler Bend Access Road and turn right. Follow the Tyler Bend Access Road 0.7 mile to the gravel road that turns left and take that road. At 0.7 mile there is a fork in the road—stay right and cross the field (stay on the road, don't drive in the grass). Once you are across the field, you have to drive across Calf Creek. If the water is up and there is any question about the safety of crossing, don't try it; come back later. Continue to follow that road until you have gone 5.7 miles from the pavement. At 5.7 miles, turn right and go 1.2 miles, where you will find another fork in the road. Go right and immediately stay right (across the field) for another 0.1 mile where the road will turn left and go into the woods. Once the road goes into the woods, it is only another 0.1 mile to the parking area. Once in the woods, the road can get really bad. If you are not in a GOOD four-wheel drive, you may want to think about parking just off the road and walking the rest of the way, especially if it has rained recently. From the parking area, the river is just down the hill. The trail is obvious.

On your way in to this one, there is one of the best views on this section of the Buffalo River (see photo on page 13), near what is known as the "Tie Slide." At 3.7 miles from the pavement, you can see where folks have been parking. Park and walk over to the bluff and have a look. Be very careful, as these are extremely high bluffs, probably not the best place to take smaller children.

If you have the *National Geographic Trails Illustrated* maps of the Buffalo River, take a look at the drawing on the cover of the East Half Map—this is the spot depicted. It is a great place to stop for a picnic lunch or just to enjoy the view.

Emergency: Searcy County Sheriff, 870–448–2340

Love-Hensley Hole, Buffalo River

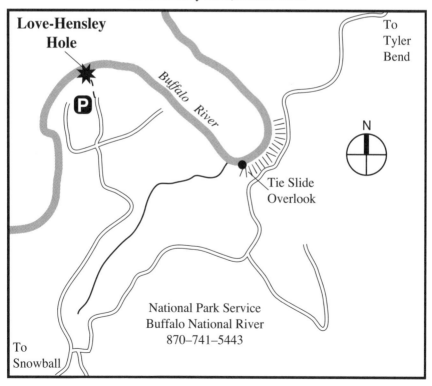

#31 Fishtrap

Buffalo River, Searcy County, Arkansas

Agency: National Park Service, Buffalo National River
Nearby community or landmark: St. Joe, Arkansas
GPS: N: 35°58'49" W: 92°47'30"
Access: Vehicle
Day Use Fee: None
Facilities: None
Activities: • swimming • fishing • canoeing
Alerts: Respect the fields

Fishtrap is a nice little hole of water that is just upstream from the mouth of Calf Creek. It is also sometimes called Arnold Bend (actually a long bend in the river is called Arnold Bend, but I have heard this hole of water called that too) or Goat Bluff (the name of a bluff at one end of the hole).

It is kind of out-of-the-way, but not too difficult to reach. You do have to take roads that cross farm fields so be sure and stay on the road.

From St. Joe, Arkansas, go south on Highway 65 for 5.2 miles and turn right onto the Tyler Bend Access Road. Follow that paved road 0.7 mile and turn left onto a dirt road—reset your trip meter here. Follow that road (taking the right at the fork at 0.7 mile) for 2.0 miles and turn right. Follow that road across the fields toward the river. Go as far upstream as the road does and park at the end by the canebreak. Follow the path through the cane to the river.

Emergency: Searcy County Sheriff, 870–448–2340

Fishtrap, Buffalo River

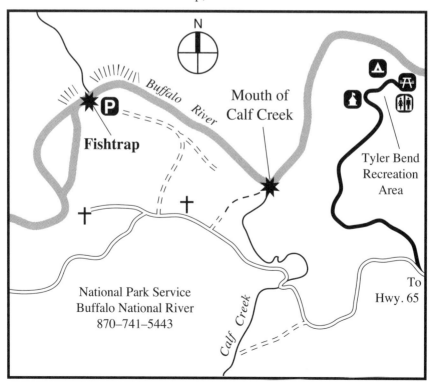

N

Buffalo River

Mouth of
Calf Creek

Fishtrap

Tyler Bend
Recreation
Area

National Park Service
Buffalo National River
870–741–5443

Calf Creek

To
Hwy. 65

#25 Mouth of Calf Creek

Buffalo River, Searcy County, Arkansas

Agency: National Park Service, Buffalo National River
Nearby community or landmark: St. Joe, Arkansas
GPS Information: N: 35°58'44" W: 92°46'21"
Access: Short hike
Day Use Fee: None
Facilities: None
Activities: • swimming • hiking • canoeing • fishing • hunting • horseback riding
Alerts: None

Calf Creek runs into the Buffalo River about a mile upstream from Tyler Bend, along the way passing near the historic community of Snowball, Arkansas. It empties into the river just upstream from a nice bluff and some great smallmouth fishing.

This is another hole that you have to cross some hay fields to get to. There is more than one way in to this one, but varying conditions will rule some of them out at times. The directions given here will call for a little walking. You should be able to reach it via this route at any time.

To reach the Mouth of Calf Creek from St. Joe, Arkansas, go south on Highway 65 for 5.2 miles to the Tyler Bend Access Road and turn right. Follow the Tyler Bend Access Road 0.7 mile to the gravel road that turns left and take that road. At 0.7 mile there is a fork in the road—stay right and cross the field (stay on the road, don't drive in the grass). Once you are across the field, you have to drive across Calf Creek. If the water is up and there is any question about the safety of crossing, don't try it—come back later. At 1.6 miles (from the pavement) you will see a road on your right with a cable across it—park nearby but don't block the road.

On foot, follow the cabled road through the fields until it comes out in a large open field. Look a little to your right and you should see a bluff, which will let you know you are on the right track. About half-way across the field (after it flattens out below a small hill), take the road that goes right. Follow that road as it takes you to the top of a creek bank and will run alongside the creek and into the woods. Once in the woods, you are just a few yards from the river. Once at the river, Calf Creek flows in from your right.

This is a great little spot to visit. It is somewhat secluded and very scenic. One of the best times to visit is later in the summer when the water levels are too low to float, and you are much more likely to have it to yourself. If you are there during good floating conditions, there will be canoes by most of the day.

The upper part of the hole is in a natural bend in the river, just below a shoal. The bottom is mostly soft and sandy. These make for great swimming conditions, but can also tend to make trees and debris wash in. Just keep an eye open, so you don't get tangled.

Emergency: Searcy County Sheriff, 870–448–2340

Mouth of Calf Creek, Buffalo River

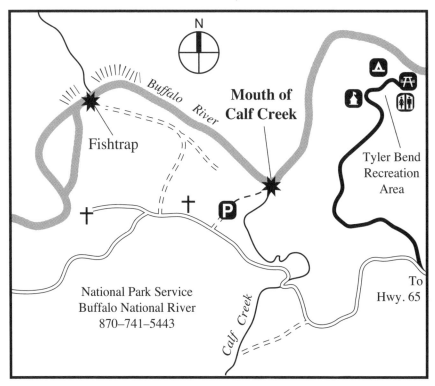

N

Buffalo River

Fishtrap

Mouth of Calf Creek

Tyler Bend Recreation Area

P

National Park Service
Buffalo National River
870–741–5443

Calf Creek

To Hwy. 65

#46 Tyler Bend
Buffalo River, Searcy County, Arkansas

Agency: National Park Service, Buffalo National River
Nearby community or landmark: St. Joe, Arkansas
GPS: N: 35°59'21" W: 92°46'03"
Access: Vehicle
Day Use Fees: None
Facilities: • modern campground • picnic tables • fire grates • drinking water available year round • flush toilets • dump station available April-October • picnic pavilion available by reservation • showers • amphitheater • handicapped accessible • pay phone
Activities: • swimming • fishing • camping • picnicking • hiking • canoeing • ranger-led activities
Alerts: None

Tyler Bend is a great campground on the Buffalo National River that is also home to the Middle Buffalo Ranger Station, all kinds of great facilities and a very neat Visitor Center/Gift Shop. Tyler Bend is a popular access point for canoers, especially those wanting to camp in a nice campground on their trip.

From Harrison, Arkansas, go south on Highway 65 for 29 miles to the Tyler Bend turnoff (you'll see the large brown Park Service Access sign—just a few miles south of St. Joe, Arkansas), where you will turn right. Follow the paved road for 2.2 miles into the park. Just follow the signs to the swimming hole, Visitors Center, registration station, or whatever you are looking for.

Emergency: Searcy County Sheriff, 870–448–2340

Tyler Bend, Buffalo River

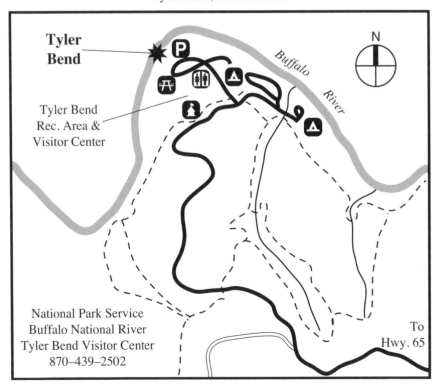

Tyler Bend

Tyler Bend
Rec. Area &
Visitor Center

Buffalo River

N

National Park Service
Buffalo National River
Tyler Bend Visitor Center
870–439–2502

To
Hwy. 65

#44 Shine Eye
Buffalo River, Searcy County, Arkansas

Agency: National Park Service, Buffalo National River
Nearby community or landmark: St. Joe, Arkansas
GPS: N: 35°59'17' W: 92°44'04"
Access: Vehicle
Day Use Fee: None
Facilities: None
Activities: • swimming • canoeing • hiking • primitive camping • hunting • fishing
Alerts: Some current at the upper end

Shine Eye is one of those places that is close to a couple of popular recreation areas (Tyler Bend and Gilbert), but is still somewhat secluded. It is more popular with locals than "tourists." This is also a popular spot to stop and swim while floating the Buffalo River.

This is a nice large swimming hole with a huge gravel bar and a neat bluff across the river. The current at the upper end of the swimming hole can be a little swift, so watch yourself (and especially the kids) in that area. There are some large boulders underwater that could cause some serious damage if you happened to jump on one of them.

To find Shine Eye from St. Joe, Arkansas, go south on Highway 65 for 4 miles. Just before you cross the bridge spanning the Buffalo River, turn left onto the side road. Follow that road 0.9 mile to the parking area. The trail is apparent at the end of the parking area. Follow it to the river just down the hill.

Emergency: Searcy County Sheriff, 870–448–2340

Shine Eye, Buffalo River

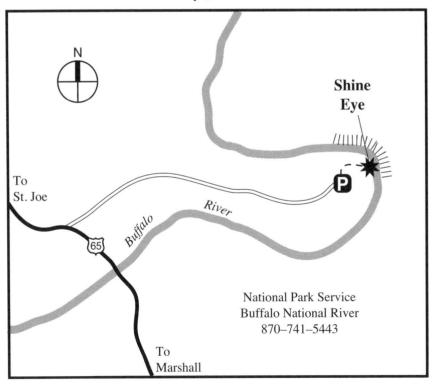

#33 Gilbert

Buffalo River, Searcy County, Arkansas

Agency: National Park Service, Buffalo National River
Nearby community or landmark: Gilbert, Arkansas
GPS: N: 35°59'10" W: 92°42'55"
Access: Vehicle
Day Use Fee: None
Facilities: • nearby cabins • general store • restaurant • pay phone
Activities: • swimming • fishing • canoeing • dining • lodging
Alerts: None

Gilbert is another one where the swimming hole is not exactly terrific, but the little town of Gilbert (population 33) is worth the trip. The river is long and shallow here, which makes for a great place to bring little ones.

The big draw here is the town. The Gilbert General Store (**www.gilbertstore.com**, 870–439–2888) is over 100 years old and still has many antique fixtures and displays. They also have cabin and canoe rentals, guesthouses and other services.

Just up the road is the Riverside Kitchen and Cottages (870–439–2288). I highly recommend you try this place, but bring your appetite. One of the lovely ladies working there told me I could show up hungry, but if I left hungry it was my own fault! I'll bet when you leave, hunger won't be an issue.

The community of Gilbert is a quaint little place, with a colorful history, that got its start in the late 1800's. Back then it was a main stop for the Missouri and North Arkansas Railroad. Trains would stop there and pick up timber that had been floated down river for later use as railroad ties.

In the 1920's, Gilbert became a religious communal settlement under the direction of the Reverend John A. Battenfield. Battenfield led his followers to Gilbert to prepare for a worldwide war between the Catholics and the Protestants that would destroy the world, as they knew it. After the war failed to come to pass, Battenfield tried to save face by bringing a dead member of the community back to life. This too failed to happen and Battenfield suffered a nervous breakdown and later failed to return from a "mission." Some of the members left the area, but some remained. They apparently found the Promised Land they had moved here in search of, even if the rest of Battenfield's prophecies never came to be.

Gilbert peaked with a population of about 333 people at one time. It is the closest town to the Buffalo River and is on the National Register of Historic Places. The community throws a big shindig each year to celebrate "Gilbert Homecoming." It is also touted as the coldest spot in Arkansas, but that shouldn't be a problem if you're there to swim.

From Harrison, Arkansas, go south on Highway 65 for 26.3 miles to the intersection of Highway 333 (you'll see Ferguson's Country Store and Restaurant at the intersection and Coursey's Smoked Meats just south). Turn left onto Highway 333 and travel 3.3 miles into the "town" of Gilbert. At the "T" intersection, turn right. Go straight ahead about 0.1 mile to the river. Swim anywhere along the gravel bar.

Emergency: Searcy County Sheriff, 870–448–2340

Gilbert, Buffalo River

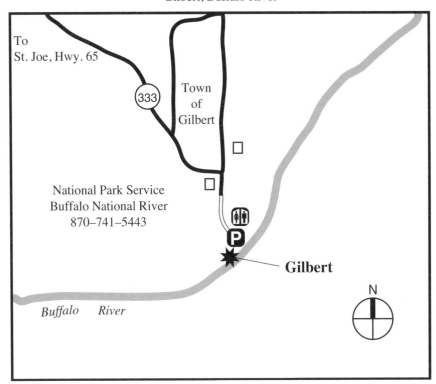

To
St. Joe, Hwy. 65

333

Town
of
Gilbert

National Park Service
Buffalo National River
870–741–5443

Gilbert

Buffalo   River

N

#29 Dillards Ferry

Buffalo River, Marion County, Arkansas

Agency: National Park Service, Buffalo National River
Nearby community or landmark: Yellville, Arkansas
GPS: N: 36°04'02" W: 92°34'40"
Access: Vehicle
Day Use Fee: None
Facilities: • restrooms • parking area
Activities: • swimming • canoeing • fishing • picnicking
Alerts: None

Dillards Ferry is also known simply as Highway 14 Bridge. As the latter implies, this area is where Highway 14 crosses the Buffalo River, which makes for very easy access. Of course, this also makes for highway noise coming from the bridge. Dillards Ferry is also a popular canoe access point, which can sometimes make it a busy place.

The swimming hole is just a long, relatively shallow stretch of river. There are no really deep places, but this is another great spot for the kids. If you are looking for an out-of-the-way place or deep water, this isn't it. But if you're looking for some easily accessible place to cool your heels while the kids splash and play, it may be for you.

Take Highway 14 south out of Yellville, Arkansas. Follow it 15.9 miles to the bridge. After you cross the bridge, turn left and follow the road back under the bridge. You will see a parking area on the left, where the road curves right. The river is just to your right.

The gravel bar is long and inviting, but can tend to get you stuck. If you don't have four-wheel drive (or even if you do), be careful about driving on it. You may just want to use the parking area and walk down.

Emergency: Marion County Sheriff, 870–449–4236

Dillards Ferry, Buffalo River

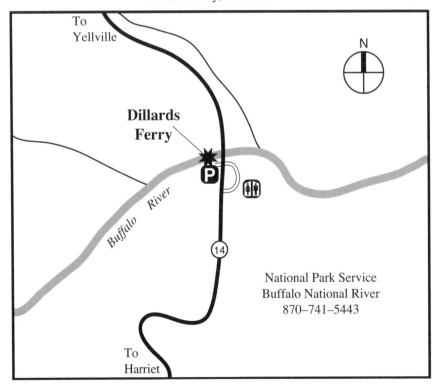

#24 Buffalo Point
Buffalo River, Marion County, Arkansas

Agency: National Park Service, Buffalo National River
Nearby community or landmark: Yellville, Arkansas
GPS: N: 36°04'26" W: 92°33'20"
Access: Vehicle
Day Use Fee: None
Facilities: • camping areas • visitor center • information stations • restrooms • showers • changing stations • canoe launch • refreshment machines • cabins • restaurant • pay phone • picnic areas • pavilion • amphitheater • hiking trails • water • dump station
Activities: • swimming • fishing • hiking • camping • canoeing • dining • lodging • ranger–led activities
Alerts: None

Buffalo Point is another all–in–one place to visit. There are some really nice campsites here; some even have water to them. There is a nice ranger station (870–449–4311), some old CCC cabins (plus some newer ones) and a restaurant with one of the best views in the country (the food and personalities are great too). For information on the cabins (March through November) or the restaurant, call Buffalo Point Concession at 870–449–6206.

The swimming hole is a nice long, deep hole of water with a huge, beautiful gravel bar on one side and a massive bluff on the other. It can tend to get a little crowded on busy weekends, partly because of the campground and canoe put–in and partly because it is just such a nice, easy-to-get-to place.

There are also some great hiking trails here. If you like hiking and unusual places, don't miss a hike into Indian Rockhouse. Indian Rockhouse is a large overhang/cave at the base of a large bluff. In one corner is a large hole all the way through the ceiling of the overhang where you can sit back and watch the sky above. In the other corner, a creek runs from the cave, several feet below where you stand, through the rocks and out the front. Use caution here, the creek can rise quickly and trap unsuspecting explorers. Others have drowned here recently. For great directions to the Indian Rockhouse Cave, check out Tim Ernst's *Arkansas Hiking Trails,* his *Buffalo River Hiking Trails*, or Pam Ernst's *Arkansas Dayhikes* guidebooks. If you don't have them before you make it to Buffalo Point, they are available at the Ranger Station.

To find Buffalo Point, take Highway 14 south from Yellville, Arkansas. Go 14.1 miles to Highway 268 (watch for brown river access signs). Turn left on Highway 268 and follow it to the park. Once inside the park, just follow the signs. The swimming area is by the canoe launch.

Emergency: Marion County Sheriff, 870–449–4236

Buffalo Point, Buffalo River

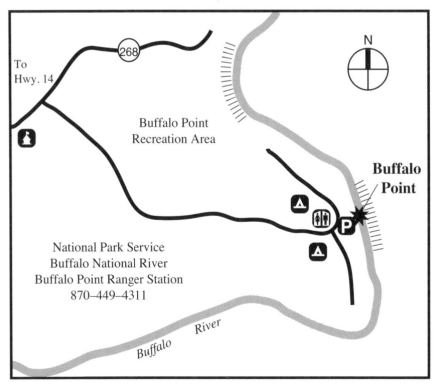

To Hwy. 14

268

Buffalo Point
Recreation Area

Buffalo
Point

National Park Service
Buffalo National River
Buffalo Point Ranger Station
870–449–4311

Buffalo River

#43 Rush

Buffalo River, Marion County, Arkansas

Agency: National Park Service, Buffalo National River
Nearby community or landmark: Yellville, Arkansas
GPS: N: 36°07'30" W: 92°32'55"
Access: Vehicle
Day Use Fee: None
Facilities: • pavilion • portable toilets • basic camping
Activities: • swimming • fishing • camping • canoeing • hiking
Alerts: None

Rush is one of the Park Service access points to the Buffalo, but is still out-of-the-way enough not to easily get crowded. The swimming here is not as good as other areas, but it is a nice, wide spot. The water is also fairly deep and is clean.

The Rush area is an old zinc and lead mining town and is worth the trip, even if you don't intend to swim. Some of the historical buildings still stand and can be seen on the trip in. There are also some interesting pieces of equipment and other treasures to be found while hiking in the area, as well as a number of old mines — never enter any of the mines though—you may never come out!

To reach Rush, go south on Highway 14 from Yellville, Arkansas, for 11.5 miles to County Road MC6035. Turn left on the county road and go 5.4 miles to the river access, following the signs. The swimming hole is just down the hill.

Emergency: Marion County Sheriff, 870–449–4236

Rush, Buffalo River

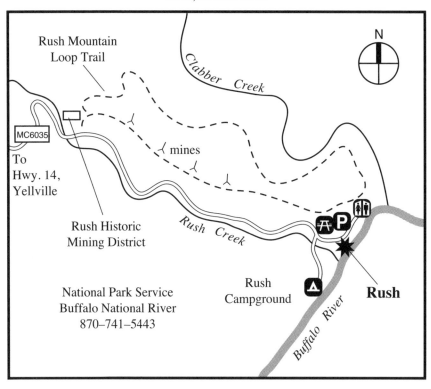

Rush Mountain
Loop Trail

Clabber Creek

N

MC6035

To
Hwy. 14,
Yellville

mines

Rush Creek

Rush Historic
Mining District

Rush
Campground

Rush

National Park Service
Buffalo National River
870–741–5443

Buffalo River

Missouri Swimming Holes

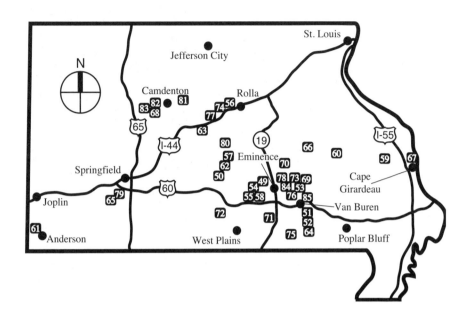

What a great time I had with our neighbors to the north. I had spent a lot of time in Missouri over the years, but not much of it was "off the beaten path." Getting to explore the out-of-the-way places and discover many of the things the state has to offer was a great thrill. Missouri has some very unique places, and her people should be proud!

For more information go to:
Ozark National Scenic Riverways—**www.nps.gov/ozar/**
Mark Twain National Forest—**www.fs.fed.us/r9/marktwain/**
Missouri State Parks—**www.mostateparks.com/**
Missouri Department of Conservation—**www.conservation.state.mo.us/**

#61 Dabbs Greer/Town Hole

Indian Creek, McDonald County, Missouri

Agency: Missouri Department of Conservation
Nearby community or landmark: Anderson, Missouri
GPS: N: 36°38'59" W: 94°26'34"
Access: Vehicle
Day Use Fee: None
Facilities: • picnic tables • vault toilets • basketball court
Activities: • swimming • fishing • picnicking • sports
Alerts: None

Dabbs Greer access to Indian Creek is a Missouri Department of Conservation-owned area that is smack in the middle of the town of Anderson, Missouri. It is also known locally as "Town Hole" for obvious reasons.

To be located in town, this is a nice little swimming hole, with easy access and other things to do. There is a nice little bluff across the creek from the parking area with neat homes on top.

The Dabbs Greer/Town Hole is easy to find. Take Highway 59 into Anderson to the downtown area and go east on Main Street for about a block and a half, then look to your right. The parking is behind the post office. The swimming hole is just below the parking area.

Andy Ostmeyer with the *Joplin Globe* told me about this one and he was right on the money. It's a great spot to visit.

Emergency: McDonald County Sheriff, 417–223–4319

Dabbs Greer/Town Hole, Indian Creek

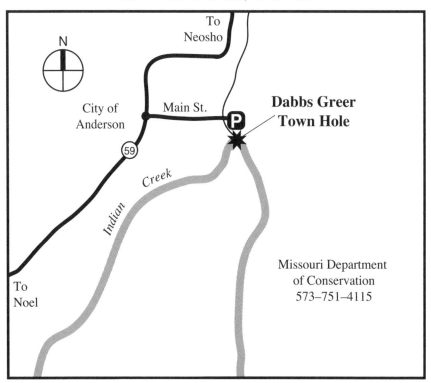

To
Neosho

N

City of
Anderson

Main St.

**Dabbs Greer
Town Hole**

P

59

Indian
Creek

To
Noel

Missouri Department
of Conservation
573–751–4115

#65 Hooten Town

James River, Stone County, Missouri

Agency: Missouri Department of Conservation
Nearby community or landmark: Nixa, Missouri
GPS: N: 36°56'23" W: 93°23'11"
Access: Vehicle
Day Use Fee: None
Facilities: • boat launch • campground nearby
Activities: • swimming • fishing • boating • camping nearby
Alerts: None

Hooten Town is another Department of Conservation access point that is also popular for swimming. It is a little out-of-the-way, yet easy to reach via a pleasant and scenic drive. There is a campground just down the river.

From Nixa, Missouri, take Highway 14 west to the edge of town and turn left (south) onto Highway M. Go 7 miles to Highway U. Take Highway U for 1.4 miles to Hooten Town Road, where you will go left. Travel 0.5 mile and turn left, then immediately left again. Most of the swimming takes place by the boat launch or under the bridge.

Emergency: Stone County Sheriff, 417–357–6117

Hooten Town, James River

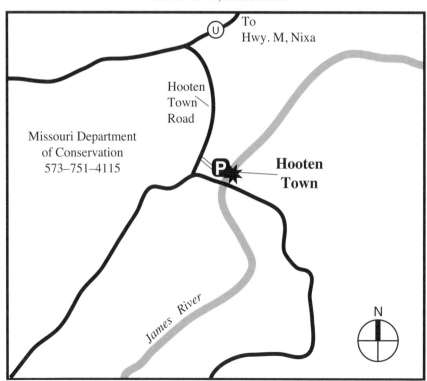

To
Hwy. M, Nixa

U

Hooten
Town
Road

Missouri Department
of Conservation
573–751–4115

P **Hooten
Town**

James River

N

#79 Shelvin Rock
James River, Christian County, Missouri

Agency: Missouri Department of Conservation
Nearby community or landmark: Nixa, Missouri
GPS: N: 36°59'40" W: 93°22'08"
Access: Vehicle
Day Use Fee: None
Facilities: None
Activities: • swimming • fishing • canoeing
Alerts: None

Shelvin Rock is a Missouri Department of Conservation access point for the James River; it is a quiet, clean place to take the kids. There are no facilities there, except a gravel boat ramp and some parking. There is plenty of slow, shallow water for the little guys to play in.

The afternoon that Susan Wade with the Springfield, Missouri Convention and Visitor's Bureau took me out there, the only folks around were Dennis Middleton and his son, out for an evening of fishing. Susan is a brave soul; she spent an entire day with me, chasing swimming holes. She knows a lot about Springfield and the surrounding area. If you need further information, contact her or one of her colleagues through their website, **www.springfieldmo.org** or at 800–678–8767.

To reach Shelvin Rock from the intersections of Highways 160 and 14 in Nixa, Missouri, go west on Highway 14 a short distance to Highway M and turn left (south). Go south on Highway M a few miles to Shelvin Rock Road, which is located right at the Christian and Stone County line. Turn right (west) onto Shelvin Rock Road and go 1.5 miles and turn left into the parking area. The swimming area is located just below the parking area.

Emergency: Christian County Sheriff, 417–581–2332

Shelvin Rock, James River

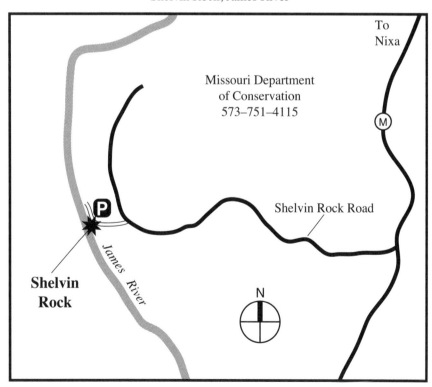

To
Nixa

Missouri Department
of Conservation
573–751–4115

M

Shelvin Rock Road

P

James River

**Shelvin
Rock**

N

#83 Tunnel Dam Low Water Bridge

Niangua River, Camden County, Missouri

Agency: Camden County, Missouri
Nearby community or landmark: Camdenton, Missouri
GPS: N: 37°56'18" W: 92°52'31"
Access: Vehicle
Day Use Fee: None
Facilities: None
Activities: • swimming • fishing
Alerts: None

This hole of water is in the county road right-of-way on the road to Lake Niangua. It's on the Niangua River, just outside the neat old community of Edith, Missouri. The swimming hole is surrounded by private property that is marked, so be sure not to trespass or park in any way that interferes.

From the intersection of Highways 5 and 54 in Camdenton, Missouri, go west on Highway 54 for 8.8 miles to the junction of Highways J and U. Reset your trip meter here. Go left on Highway U and then immediately right. Continue on and at 2.8 miles you are in Edith, Missouri. Be sure and look over at the great old rock building on your left and if you have time, stop and look at the way the outhouses are set up. I think you'll agree that equal rights for the sexes are not in play here. The ladies have a nice, white, two-door, duplex style outhouse with a privacy fence and lights. The men have an old, rustic wood structure behind the ladies' facility that is not quite on par with the ladies'. I guess the building fund was running short before that was replaced.

From Edith, Missouri, turn right onto Whistle Road and go 0.6 mile to Tunnel Dam Road, turn left, cross the bridge and park in the wide place on the left-hand side of the road. The swimming area is located near the parking area towards the bridge.

Emergency: Camden County Sheriff, 573–346–2243

Tunnel Dam Low Water Bridge, Niangua River

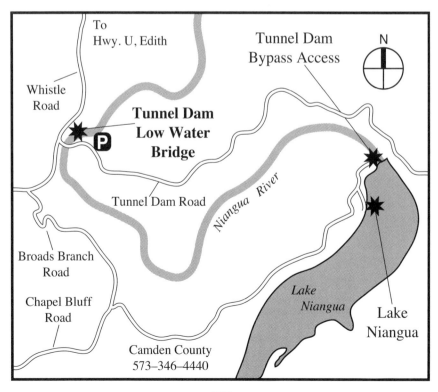

#68 Lake Niangua
Lake Niangua, Camden County, Missouri

Agency: Sho-Me Power Company
Nearby community or landmark: Camdenton, Missouri
GPS: N: 37°56'03" W: 92°51'06"
Access: Vehicle
Day Use Fee: None
Facilities: None
Activities: • swimming • fishing • boating
Alerts: None

Lake Niangua is a three-mile-long impoundment of the Niangua River that was built in 1929 by Sho-Me Power Company. The small hydroelectric dam that holds the lake is still in use today. Lake Niangua is also a great place to wet a hook, especially for some slab crappies.

To reach Lake Niangua from the intersection of Highways 5 and 54 in Camdenton, Missouri, go west on Highway 54 for 8.8 miles. This will be the junction of Highways J and U. Go left on Highway U and then turn immediately right. Follow that 2.8 miles to the old community of Edith. In Edith, turn right onto Whistle Road and go 0.8 mile to Broads Branch Road and go left. Follow Broads Branch Road another 0.8 mile to Chapel Bluff Road and again turn left following that road 1.4 miles (stay straight at the 0.8 mile intersection). The last part of the road will wind through some fields and end up at the parking area.

Emergency: Camden County Sheriff, 573–346–2243

Lake Niangua

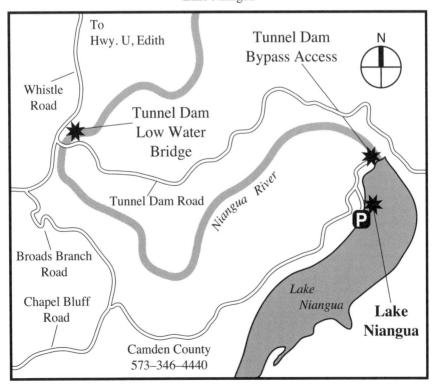

To
Hwy. U, Edith

Tunnel Dam
Bypass Access

N

Whistle
Road

Tunnel Dam
Low Water
Bridge

Tunnel Dam Road

Niangua River

P

Broads Branch
Road

Chapel Bluff
Road

Lake
Niangua

**Lake
Niangua**

Camden County
573–346–4440

#82 Tunnel Dam Bypass Access
Niangua River, Camden County, Missouri

Agency: Sho-Me Power Company
Nearby community or landmark: Camdenton, Missouri
GPS: N: 37°56'14" W: 92°51'06"
Access: Vehicle
Day Use Fee: None
Facilities: None
Activities: • swimming • fishing • canoeing
Alerts: This can apparently be quite the party spot, so watch for glass, etc… And stay off the dam.

This is a unique spot if you are looking for something a little different. It is the base of an old dam that forms Lake Niangua (a three-mile-long power company lake). The dam is not very large and is built into the hillside. The water flows over the top of the dam and cascades down the stair-stepped front, making it quite scenic. Also notable is that the dam was built about 1929 and is still in use.

This particular spot was chosen (and named) for a cave that engineers located on the site. Originally, a power generating dam was built near the top of the cave and the "tunnel" was used for the overflow of the water. When the present dam was built, it was located about 75 feet upstream from the cave entrance (which had been artificially enlarged). Plans to use the cave as a tailrace were later abandoned after several branches of the cave were discovered. The view from the ridgetop above the dam is pretty spectacular as well.

To find this place from the intersection of Highways 5 and 54 in Camdenton, Missouri, go west on Highway 54 for 8.8 miles. This will be the junction of Highways J and U. Go left on Highway U and then turn immediately right. Follow that 2.8 miles to the old community of Edith (there are a couple of great old buildings here). In Edith, turn right onto Whistle Road and go 0.8 mile to Broads Branch Road and go left. Follow Broads Branch Road another 0.8 mile to Chapel Bluff Road and again turn left following that road 1.3 miles (stay straight at the 0.8 mile intersection). At 1.3 miles, turn left and follow it 0.2 mile to the parking. The swimming hole is right there.

As I mentioned earlier, this can apparently be a party place at night. And it is obvious there are some real jerks that party there and don't know how to clean up after themselves. It is a very scenic and unique place, but can sometimes be a little trashy because of a few idiots. Have the kids wear their shoes and watch out for glass and other hazards. You should probably avoid trying your new climbing shoes on the dam, as well.

Emergency: Camden County Sheriff, 573–346–2243

Tunnel Dam Bypass, Niangua River

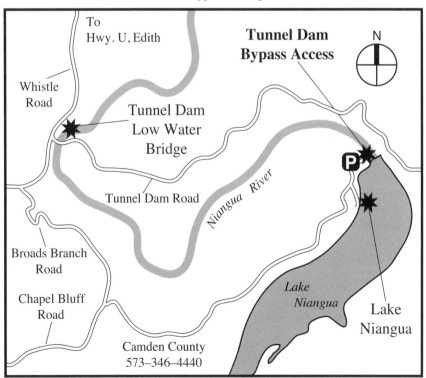

To
Hwy. U, Edith

**Tunnel Dam
Bypass Access**

N

Whistle
Road

Tunnel Dam
Low Water
Bridge

P

Tunnel Dam Road

Niangua River

Broads Branch
Road

Chapel Bluff
Road

*Lake
Niangua*

Lake
Niangua

Camden County
573–346–4440

#81 Swinging Bridges

Grand Auglaize Creek, Miller County, Missouri

Agency: Missouri Department of Natural Resources, State Parks
Nearby community or landmark: Osage Beach, Missouri
GPS: N: 38°04'41" W: 92°31'39"
Access: Vehicle
Day Use Fee: None
Facilities: • primitive campsites • vault toilet • boat launch
Activities: • swimming • fishing • camping • boating • canoeing • historical significance
Alerts: None

Swinging Bridges is a quiet, out-of-the-way place that is not too far from bustling Lake of the Ozarks. In fact it is within the boundaries of Lake of the Ozarks State Park.

It is named after the wood-planked swinging bridges in the area; one is visible from the swimming hole. A man named Joe Dice, from Warsaw, Missouri, built the bridge in 1929 or 1930. Mr. Dice left school in the fourth grade with bad eyesight and went on to design and build about 40 suspension bridges in Missouri, several of which are still in use. Instead of high tech equipment, Mr. Dice used a ball of twine for determining distances and the amount of curve, then used horses, mules and men for the rest. Area farms were the source of gravel and timber. Many of his bridges are still testament to his skill. Not bad for a fourth grade dropout.

From the intersection of Highways 54 and 42 in Osage Beach, Missouri, go south from town on Highway 42 east for 9.1 miles. Turn right onto Lake Road 42–18/Swinging Bridges Road, and reset your trip meter here. Go 1.8 miles and just after crossing the first bridge, take a right at the fork. Cross the second bridge (it's safe, although it may look a little rickety), and then take the first right into the parking area. The swimming area is just below you.

For more information on this area, check with Carol Zeman or one of the other fine folks at Lake of the Ozarks Convention and Visitor's Bureau, 800–FUN–LAKE or **www.funlake.com**.

Emergency: Miller County Sheriff, 573–369–2341

Swinging Bridges, Grand Auglaize Creek

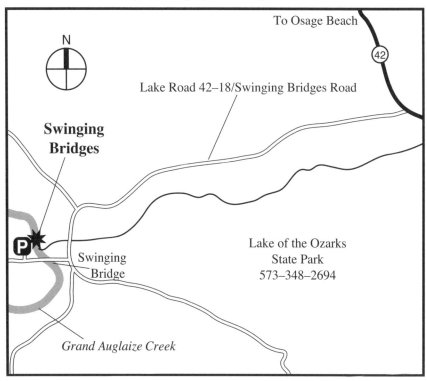

#56 Boiling Spring, Gasconade
Gasconade River, Pulaski County, Missouri

Agency: Private with public access
Nearby community or landmark: St. Robert or Fort Leonard Wood, Missouri
GPS: N: 37°53'23" W: 92°02'10"
Access: Vehicle
Day Use Fee: Yes
Facilities: • campground with electric and water hookups • flushing toilets
• pavilion • volleyball court • grills • boat ramp • pay phone
Activities: • swimming • camping • fishing • boating • picnicking
Alerts: None

Boiling Spring Campground is a quiet, clean, family-oriented campground that is actually across the Gasconade River from Boiling Spring (**www.dixoncamping.com**). A local family owns the campground, and the pride they put into it is obvious. It is not called "Boiling" Spring because the water is 212° F, but because the spring water flows up from the riverbed, causing the top of the river to look as if it is boiling.

This is a pretty stretch of river that also happens to hold some trophy fish. There is a boat ramp right at the campground if you want to give that a shot. But for swimming, the access you get and the facilities available for a dollar a day per person just can't be beat. This is not one of the places to go if you are looking for an out-of-the-way place for a wilderness experience. But if you're around Fort Leonard Wood and the kids are bugging you to take them to the river, this would sure be worth a look.

From Interstate 44, take Exit 163 and go north on Highway 28, then go 5.9 miles to Highway PP (I'm not making that up, see the picture below). Go 3.4 miles on Highway PP to the access road (you will see a sign). Turn right and follow it to the river. On the way in you will pass the information station, where you pay your day fees. You can see the river from the parking area.

Emergency: Pulaski County Sheriff, 573–774–6196

Boiling Spring, Gasconade River

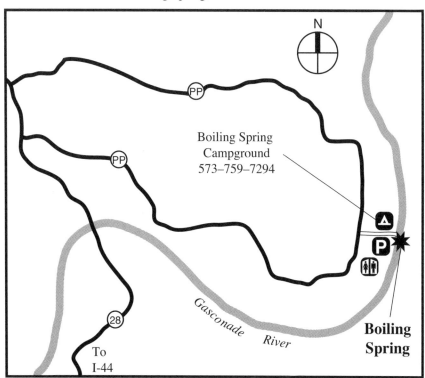

N

Boiling Spring
Campground
573–759–7294

Gasconade River

Boiling
Spring

To
I-44

#74 Riddle Bridge
Gasconade River, Pulaski County, Missouri

Agency: Missouri Department of Conservation
Nearby community or landmark: Waynesville, Missouri
GPS: N: 37°54'34" W: 92°07'56"
Access: Vehicle
Day Use Fee: None
Facilities: • boat ramp • vault toilets
Activities: • swimming • fishing • canoeing • boating
Alerts: None

Riddle Bridge is an access point to the Gasconade River not far from Waynesville, Missouri. There is a nice rock "mountain" across the river from the parking area and room for plenty of folks.

From Interstate 44 and Exit 161 in Waynesville, Missouri, go north on Highway Y. Follow Highway Y for 6.9 miles and turn left into the parking area just before the bridge.

This area is just outside Fort Leonard Wood and there are some great outdoor and historical things to see and do here. Stop in at the Pulaski County Tourism Office at 137 St. Robert Blvd. in nearby St. Robert, Missouri, and Andy Thiem and his cohorts can help you out. You could also call them toll free at 877–858–8687 or visit them on the web at **www.visitpulaskicounty.org**.

Emergency: Pulaski County Sheriff, 573–774–6196

Riddle Bridge, Gasconade River

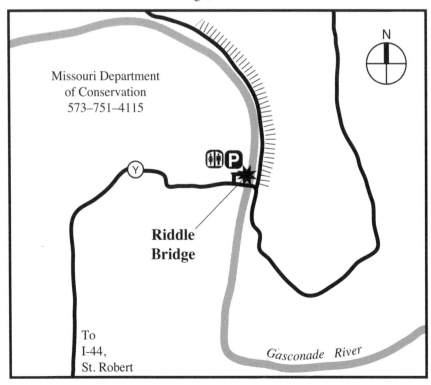

Missouri Department
of Conservation
573–751–4115

**Riddle
Bridge**

To
I-44,
St. Robert

Gasconade River

N

#77 Mouth of Roubidoux Creek

(pronounced "ruby-doo")
Gasconade River, Pulaski County, Missouri

Agency: Missouri Department of Transportation
Nearby community or landmark: Waynesville, Missouri
GPS: N: 37°51'03" W: 92°12'49"
Access: Vehicle
Day Use Fee: None
Facilities: None
Activities: • swimming • fishing • canoeing
Alerts: None

There are several swimming holes in the Ozarks that are simply "underneath the bridge." Most bridges have an access road at one end or the other that leads down to the stream the bridge spans. My observations would suggest that one of the things learned in engineering school, during "Bridges, How and Where to Build Them" class is something like; "When determining the best location for said bridge, search the area in which the road is to be built. Once you find the best swimming hole in the area, build a bridge."

The Mouth of Roubidoux Creek is one of those spots and is actually in the right-of-way of the highway. To reach it from Interstate 44 near Waynesville, Missouri, take Exit 159 and go north on 44 Business (Route 66) 1.8 miles to Highway 17. Turn right on Highway 17 and go 2.2 miles. Just before you cross the bridge, the access road turns off to the left. The swimming hole is just below you.

Emergency: Pulaski County Sheriff, 573–774–6196

Mouth of Roubidoux Creek, Gasconade River

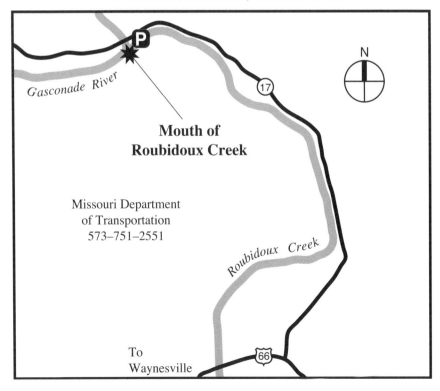

#63 Gasconade Hills
Gasconade River, Pulaski County, Missouri

Agency: Private, with public access
Nearby community or landmark: Waynesville, Missouri
GPS: N: 37°45'01" W: 92°23'50"
Access: Vehicle
Day Use Fee: Yes
Facilities: • full service campground • electric hookup • sewer • fire pits • store with bait • groceries • ice and supplies • cabins • laundromat • canoe • kayak • inner tube and johnboat rental • playground • large pool (from Memorial Day to Labor Day weekend) • game room • pay phone • modern bathhouses • L/P gas • pavilion • catering • river access • friendly staff • climate controlled meeting facility
Activities: • swimming • fishing • canoeing • boating • tubing • camping • lodging • playing
Alerts: None

Gasconade Hills is another one of the few private properties to make the book. This is a nice, full-service campground run by Bob and Pat Sutcliffe and their family. We met up with Bob while doing research for the book and we couldn't have asked for a friendlier, more helpful person.

The campground is clean and in great shape and these guys have received high marks for cleanliness and facilities in the *National Trailer Life Directory*, a highly respected camping guide. Give them a call at 573–765–3044 or visit them on the web at **www.canoemissouri.com**.

To find the campground from Interstate 44, take Exit 145 and go south on Highway AB for 0.1 mile. At the "T," turn left and go another 0.1 mile and turn right onto Spring Road. Follow that 1.2 miles to the campground. Swimming is near the canoe access or below the bridge at the end of the campground.

Emergency: Pulaski County Sheriff, 573–774–6196

Gasconade Hills, Gasconade River

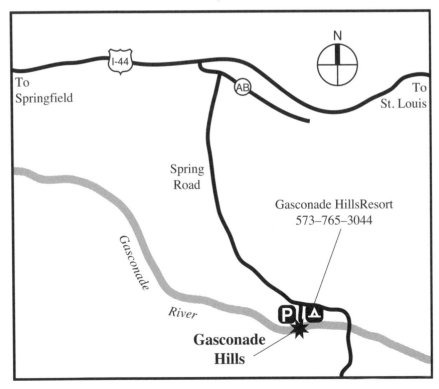

#80 Slabtown

Big Piney River, Texas County, Missouri

Agency: U.S. Forest Service, Mark Twain National Forest
Nearby community or landmark: Licking, Missouri
GPS: N: 37°33'41: W: 92°01'55"
Access: Vehicle
Day Use Fee: None
Facilities: • picnic area • primitive campground • vault toilet • hiking trail
Activities: • swimming • fishing • canoeing • hiking • camping • picnicking
Alerts: None

Slabtown is an access point for the Big Piney River that is located not too far from Licking, Missouri. There is a small open area that is designated as a primitive campground. There are vault toilets, a picnic area and a hiking trail that follows the river.

From the intersection of Highways 63 and 32 in Licking, Missouri, go west on Highway 32 for 3.8 miles to Highway N and turn right (north). Follow Highway N for 2.2 miles and turn left onto Highway AF. Follow AF for 5.5 miles to the Slabtown Access sign and turn left. Follow the access road 0.2 mile to the parking area and park by the "Bluff Trail" sign.

To reach the swimming hole, follow the trail across the small creek for about 30 yards until the trail starts to curve toward the river. Swim along the area below you.

Emergency: Texas County Sheriff, 417–967–4165

Slabtown, Big Piney River

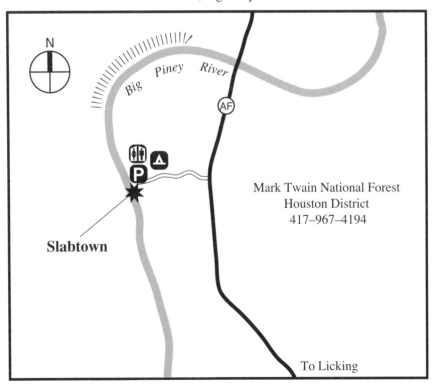

#57 Boiling Spring Hole, Big Piney

Big Piney River, Texas County, Missouri

Agency: Missouri Department of Conservation
Nearby community or landmark: Houston, Missouri
GPS: N: 37°27'41" W: 91°59'17"
Access: Vehicle
Day Use Fee: None
Facilities: • large parking area • boat ramp • picnic tables • fire pits • toilets • full service campground and resort next door
Activities: • swimming • fishing • canoeing • picnicking • nearby camping and lodging
Alerts: Private property around the spring

Boiling Spring Access is a Missouri Department of Conservation fishing access that is also a popular swimming hole with locals, canoeists and patrons of the campground and resort next door. There are picnic tables, fire pits and the like, but no camping facilities are located there. But just next door is Boiling Springs Resort. They offer full hookup campsites, basic campsites, cabins, canoe and other boat rentals and other services. I haven't met the folks, but they have plenty of information on the web at www.boilingspringsresort.com.

The access is named after a large underwater spring just upstream from the bridge. The spring puts out about 12 million gallons of water a day and since it is under a shallow part of the river, it makes the water appear as if it is boiling, but, of course, it is nowhere near 212° F!

If you find yourself at the intersection of Highways 63 and B on the north end of Houston, Missouri, head north on Highway 63. You'll travel 10.1 miles to the intersection of Highway BB and turn left (look for the access sign). Follow Highway BB for 7.7 miles and the pavement will end at the parking area. You can swim pretty much anywhere along the access, but there is usually a rope swing across from the main parking area.

Emergency: Texas County Sheriff, 417–967–4165

Boiling Spring Hole, Big Piney

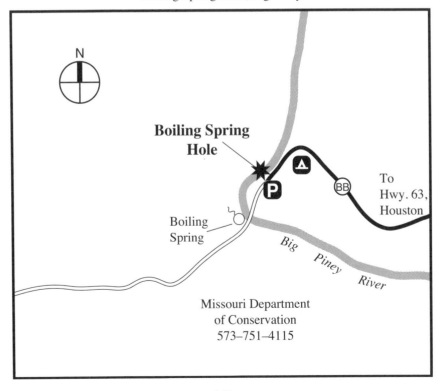

#62 Dog's Bluff
Big Piney River, Texas County, Missouri

Agency: Missouri Department of Conservation
Nearby community or landmark: Houston, Missouri
GPS: N: 37°19'36" W: 92°00'08"
Access: Vehicle
Day Use Fee: None
Facilities: • picnic tables • fire pits • boat ramp • toilets
Activities: • swimming • fishing • canoeing • picnicking
Alerts: Be careful swinging or jumping off the bluff.

Dog's Bluff is another nice, scenic spot on the Big Piney River that is just minutes out of Houston, Missouri. It is located right where the highway crosses the river, so there is some traffic noise and it could tend to get a little crowded. It is a lovely spot with a gorgeous little bluff, easy access, nice facilities, and usually a rope swing.

It's easy to find from Houston, Missouri. Just head west on Highway 17 for 3 miles until you cross the bridge over the Big Piney River. Then turn right into the parking area and the swimming hole is just below you.

Emergency: Texas County Sheriff, 417–967–4165

Dog's Bluff, Big Piney River

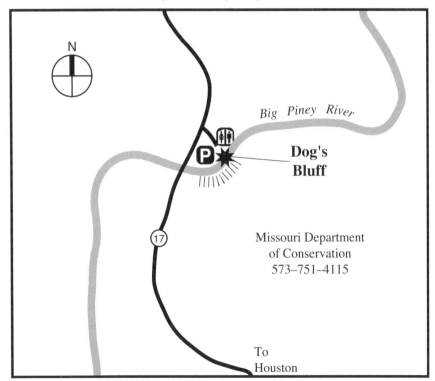

N

Big Piney River

Dog's Bluff

P

17

Missouri Department
of Conservation
573–751–4115

To
Houston

#50 Baptist Camp
Big Piney River, Texas County, Missouri

Agency: Missouri Department of Conservation
Nearby community or landmark: Houston, Missouri
GPS: N: 37°15'30" W: 92°01'07"
Access: Vehicle
Day Use Fee: None
Facilities: • picnic tables • fire pits
Activities: • swimming • fishing • canoeing • picnicking
Alerts: Private property on top of the small bluff. Watch the currents around the bridge, especially with the little ones.

Baptist Camp is a lovely spot on the Big Piney River, not far out of Houston, Missouri, that is quiet and easy to get to. It is named after a nearby Baptist summer camp that is just downstream from the access. Some beautiful, small bluffs line the west side of the swimming hole and have a few nice waterfalls when conditions are wet enough.

The Big Piney River is one of Missouri's premier fishing streams with great fishing for smallmouth bass, catfish, perch and goggle eye (rock bass). A friend, Jim Trammell, spent most of his high school years in Houston, Missouri, and has told me that he caught the biggest goggle eye he has ever seen in this very hole of water. I know, I know, a fish story; but I'll take his word for it.

To reach Baptist Camp from the intersection of Highways 63 and 17 east in Houston, go south on Highway 63 for 5 miles to Highway RA and turn right (west). Follow Highway RA for a mile to the parking area, just before the low water slab. The swimming hole is just in front of you.

There is private property on top of the bluff, so remember to respect the landowner's rights.

Emergency: Texas County Sheriff, 417–967–4165

Baptist Camp, Big Piney River

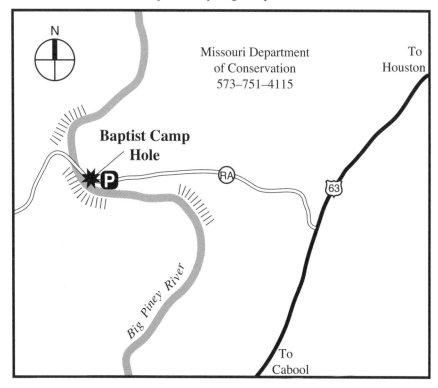

#72 Noblett Lake

Noblett Lake, Douglas County, Missouri

Agency: U.S. Forest Service, Mark Twain National Forest
Nearby community or landmark: Willow Springs, Missouri
GPS: N: 36°54'28" W: 92°06'08"
Access: Vehicle
Day Use Fee: None
Facilities: • boat ramp • restrooms • pavilions • playground • hiking trails
• grills • drinking water
Activities: • swimming • fishing • picnicking • playing • hiking • boating
Alerts: If swimming on the dam end, don't get too close.

Noblett Lake is another Forest Service lake in Missouri that is more of a fishing lake, but is a good swimming hole too, especially on the end near the dam. (Don't get too close to the dam though.)

At one time, the lake was closed to swimming due to high levels of organic growth, but that was decades ago and it is now cleaned up and ready to go. It is in a scenic area and has a nice recreation area at the opposite end of the lake from the dam.

To reach Noblett Lake from the intersection of Highways 76 and 63 in Willow Springs, Missouri, go west on Highway 76 for 7.0 miles to Highway 181 and turn left, reseting your trip meter here. Follow Highway 181 for 1.3 miles and turn left onto Highway AP and reset again. Follow Highway AP for 3 miles, turning right onto Forest Road 857. After 0.8 mile on Forest Road 857 you can either turn right on the access road and follow that to the recreation area, or you can stay straight on Forest Road 857 and follow it to the parking area near the dam.

Emergency: Douglas County Sheriff, 417–683–1020

Noblett Lake

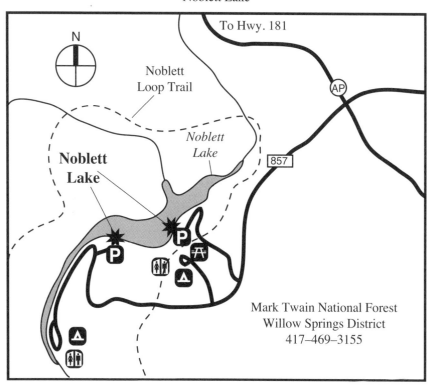

#58 Buck Hollow

Jacks Fork River, Texas County, Missouri

Agency: National Park Service, Ozark National Scenic Riverways
Nearby community or landmark: Mountain View, Missouri
GPS: N: 37°03'23" W: 91°40'04"
Access: Vehicle
Day Use Fee: None
Facilities: • canoe access • picnic area • chemical toilets
Activities: • swimming • fishing • canoeing • picnicking
Alerts: None

Buck Hollow is one of the Park Service's access points to the Jacks Fork River. There are really three swimming holes here. One is upstream of the parking, on the upriver side of the Highway 17 bridge. That hole is a nice wide swimming area with a pretty bluff across the river.

Another swimming area is just upriver of the canoe access. This one is near the end of the access road leading from the highway. It is a smaller hole with a small bluff on the far side.

The last one is just downstream of the canoe put-in. There appear to be several good swimming holes downriver, so the area may be worth some exploring to get away from the canoe access traffic. The entire area would be a great place to bring the kids.

To reach the area from Mountain View, Missouri, go east on Highway 60. Just outside the town of Mountain View, you will see Highway 17. Go north on Highway 17 until you reach the bridge spanning Jacks Fork River. At the south end of the bridge, you will see an access road to the right (east). Just follow this road a few hundred feet to the turn around. You cannot park in the turn-around, but parking is allowed between there and the highway.

Emergency: Texas County Sheriff 417–967–4165

Buck Hollow, Jacks Fork River

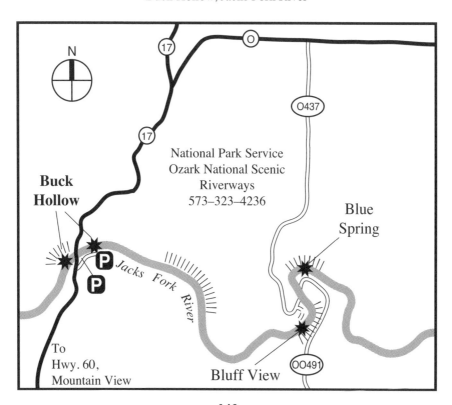

#55 Bluff View

Jacks Fork River, Shannon County, Missouri

Agency: National Park Service, Ozark National Scenic Riverways
Nearby community or landmark: Mountain View, Missouri
GPS: N: 37° 03'08" W: 91°38'18"
Access: Vehicle
Day Use Fee: None
Facilities: • picnic table • fire ring
Activities: • swimming • fishing • canoeing • picnicking
Alerts: High bluffs, be careful if you decide to jump off. Do so at your own risk. Road can get rough, so four-wheel drive is sometimes needed.

Bluff View is located just upstream a few yards from Blue Spring (see the next page), but as mentioned there, it is oftentimes not a good idea to drive across here. It is better to come into Blue Spring from the other side, as directed on that page. Bluff View is so named because of the beautiful bluffs there that daredevils like to jump off of. These bluffs are fairly high for jumping, so if you do so make sure you know what you are doing, do it SOBER and be careful! It's not a bad idea to wait until some of the locals are around and bailing off, so you can see where the safe spots are.

From the light at the intersection of Highways 17 south and 60 in Mountain View, Missouri, go east on Highway 60 for 1.5 miles and turn left (north) onto Highway 17 north. Reset and follow Highway 17 north for 5.2 miles to Highway O (Highway 17 N goes left here and Highway O goes straight). Go straight on Highway O, then reset and go 1.1 miles to Shannon County Road O-437. Turn right (south), reset and go 2.2 miles. A few yards before the road crosses the river (or the river crosses the road, depending on how you look at it) a small road turns right and into the parking area. There are two or three good places to get down to the swimming area here, so just pick one and jump in!

Emergency: Shannon County Sheriff, 573–226–3615

Bluff View, Jacks Fork River

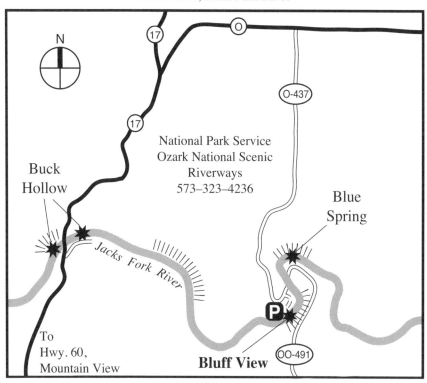

N

17

O

O-437

17

National Park Service
Ozark National Scenic
Riverways
573–323–4236

Buck
Hollow

Blue
Spring

Jacks Fork River

To
Hwy. 60,
Mountain View

P

Bluff View

OO-491

#54 Blue Spring, Jacks Fork
Jacks Fork River, Shannon County, Missouri

Agency: National Park Service, Ozark National Scenic Riverways
Nearby community or landmark: Mountain View, Missouri
GPS: N: 37°03'17" W: 91° 38' 19"
Access: Vehicle
Day Use Fee: None
Facilities: • vault toilets • picnic tables • fire rings
Activities: • swimming • fishing • canoeing • primitive camping • picnicking
Alerts: More broken glass than most places

Blue Spring on the Jacks Fork River is so named for the spring at the base of a bluff at the river's edge. Once when I was there after heavy rains, the river was up and muddy, but you could still see the blue part near the spring across the way. This is a pretty area and is actually just downstream a few yards from Bluff View, but the access road comes in from the opposite side of the river.

As mentioned in the alerts above, there seemed to be a LOT of broken glass here, much more than is usually found. It was more in the parking and picnic area and not so much on the gravel and sand bars, but keep an eye open and the shoes on the little ones. I don't know if the thugs that left it all behind just don't care if your kids, or my kids, or their kids for that matter, step on this and end up with a nasty cut or if they are just too ignorant to know better. Either way, watch your step.

From the light at the intersection of Highways 60 and 17 in Mountain View, Missouri, go east on Highway 60 for 3 miles to Highway OO and turn left (north). Reset and go 2.3 miles to where the pavement ends and turn left (west) onto Shannon County Road OO-491. Reset again and follow that road (staying left at 1.4 miles) for 2.1 miles and turn right into the parking area. The swimming hole is just below you.

If you continue past the parking area just a little ways, the road crosses the river. Just on the other side is Bluff View (see previous pages), but it is usually not advised to drive across here. Instead come in from the other side, as directed on that page.

Emergency: Shannon County Sheriff, 573–226–3615

Blue Spring, Jacks Fork River

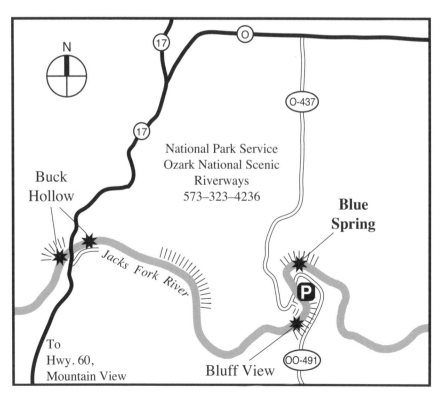

#49 Alley Spring Campground
Jacks Fork River, Shannon County, Missouri

Agency: National Park Service, Ozark National Scenic Riverways
Nearby community or landmark: Eminence, Missouri
GPS: N: 37° 09'02" W: 91°27'04"
Access: Very short hike
Day Use Fee: None
Facilities: • campground • restrooms • showers • dump station • family sites • group sites • firewood • pay phone
Activities: • swimming • canoeing • fishing • camping
Alerts: None

The Alley Spring Campground swimming hole is not far out of the neat little town of Eminence, Missouri, and is within walking distance of Alley Mill, a very picturesque spot I recommend you visit if in the area. The swimming hole here has a small bluff that folks jump off of and is popular with some of the locals.

From the intersection of Highways 19 and 106 in Eminence, Missouri, go west on Highway 106 for 5.1 miles and turn left (south) onto Shannon County Road 106-426, which is also the entrance to the campground. Reset here and go 0.5 mile on the main road through the campground and turn right onto a short dirt road, staying right at the fork. Follow this 0.1 mile to the parking area. The road has loose gravel and sand and if you don't have four-wheel drive, you probably should park and walk the 0.1 mile to the parking area.

From the left (upstream) end of the parking area, a trail takes off through the woods and downhill toward the river. Follow that trail. At the bottom of the little hill the trail will fork, the right goes to a small gravel bar and the left continues through the woods. Take the left trail until you find the hole of water with the small bluff across the way. The swimming hole is about 200 yards from the parking area.

Emergency: Shannon County Sheriff, 573–226–3615

Alley Spring Campground, Jacks Fork River

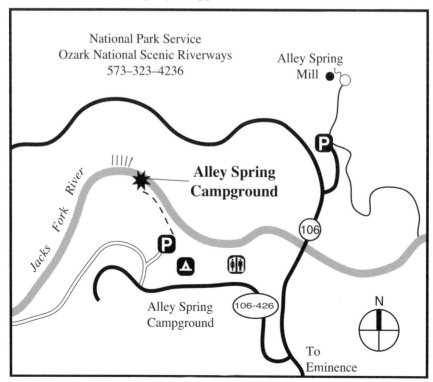

National Park Service
Ozark National Scenic Riverways
573–323–4236

Alley Spring Mill

Alley Spring Campground

Jacks Fork River

106

Alley Spring Campground

106-426

N

To Eminence

#78 Mouth of Shawnee Creek

Jacks Fork River, Shannon County, Missouri

Agency: National Park Service, Ozark National Scenic Riverways
Nearby community or landmark: Eminence, Missouri
GPS: N: 37°10'22" W: 91°18'01"
Access: Vehicle
Day Use Fee: None
Facilities: • campsites • toilets • horse and hiking trails
Activities: • swimming • canoeing • fishing • hiking • camping • horseback riding
Alerts: None

The Mouth of Shawnee Creek is a nice, secluded spot to get away to, but is not one of the better swimming holes in the area. You can camp here and not only swim, but enjoy the hiking trails and if you have horses, you can ride them as well.

To reach the parking/camping area from Eminence, Missouri, go east on Highway 106 for 2.8 miles. Turn left (north) on the dirt road at the Shawnee Creek Access sign and go 1.8 miles. You are now at the camping area and the river is straight ahead.

Emergency: Shannon County Sheriff, 573–226–3615

Mouth of Shawnee Creek, Jacks Fork River

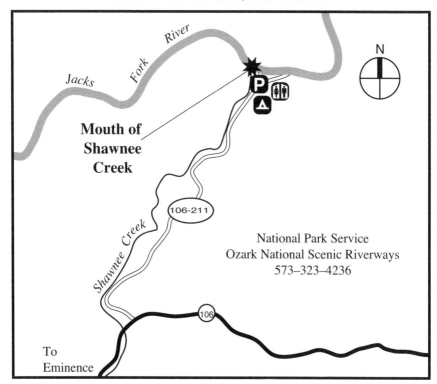

N

Jacks Fork River

Mouth of
Shawnee
Creek

106-211

Shawnee Creek

106

To
Eminence

National Park Service
Ozark National Scenic Riverways
573–323–4236

84 Two Rivers
Current and Jacks Fork Rivers, Shannon County, Missouri

Agency: National Park Service, Ozark National Scenic Riverways
Nearby community or landmark: Eminence, Missouri
GPS: N: 37°11'26" W: 91°16'34"
Access: Vehicle
Day Use Fee: None
Facilities: • campground • area canoe rentals • boat launch • bathrooms • hot showers • store • pay phone
Activities: • swimming • camping • fishing • canoeing • hiking • boating
Alerts: None

Two Rivers is the confluence of the Current and Jacks Fork Rivers. There is a really nice, full-service campground with great access to the water. You can rent a canoe, launch a boat or just spend the day in the camper. There are nearby cabin rentals and private campgrounds as well.

To reach Two Rivers from Eminence, Missouri, go east on Highway 106 for 5.2 miles to Highway V. Turn left (north) on Highway V and go 2.9 miles into the campground. Once at the campground, you can either hike down the trail a short distance to the river, or you can keep going and take the first left to the river. The road to the vehicle access is posted as "Four Wheel Drive Only," but sometimes you can make it in a regular vehicle. It would be wise to check the conditions before driving down in anything but a 4 X 4.

Emergency: Shannon County Sheriff, 573–226–3615

Two Rivers, Current and Jacks Fork Rivers

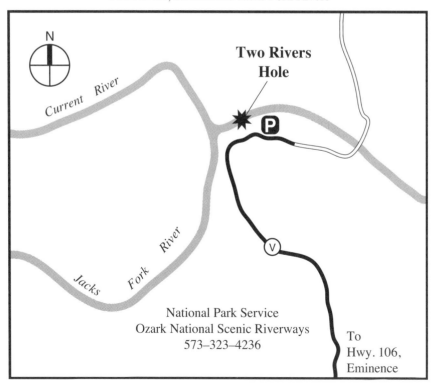

National Park Service
Ozark National Scenic Riverways
573–323–4236

#73 Powder Mill

Current River, Shannon County, Missouri

Agency: National Park Service, Ozark National Scenic Riverways
Nearby community or landmark: Eminence, Missouri
GPS: N: 37°10'55" W: 91°10'33"
Access: Vehicle
Day Use Fee: None
Facilities: • campground • picnic facilities • water • hiking trails • ranger station • pay phone
Activities: • swimming • camping • picnicking • hiking • floating • fishing
Alerts: Watch the current here. Be sure and swim well upstream of the shoal.

This is a very nice campground and access area. The camping and recreation facilities are first rate and would be a good place to spend the weekend with the family. There isn't a classic, defined "hole," but the river is wide and deep enough to swim and the gravel bar is super. As mentioned above, be aware of the current near the shoal and keep the kids well upriver of it.

To reach the area from Eminence, Missouri, go east on Highway 106 for 13.2 miles. You will cross the bridge spanning the Current River, then turn right at the sign. Just follow that road about a half mile to the river.

Emergency: Shannon County Sheriff, 573–226–3615

Powder Mill, Current River

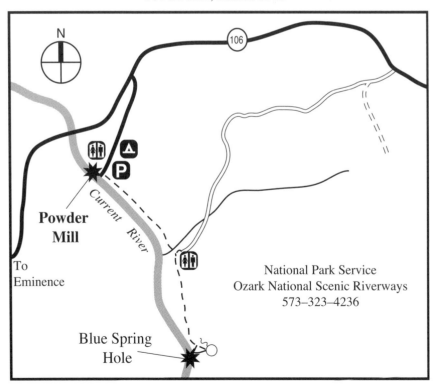

#53 Blue Spring Hole, Current River

Current River, Shannon County, Missouri

Agency: National Park Service, Ozark National Scenic Riverways
Nearby community or landmark: Eminence, Missouri
GPS: N: 37°09'59" W: 91°09'54"
Access: Short hike
Day Use Fee: None
Facilities: • picnic tables • toilets
Activities: • swimming • hiking • picnicking
Alerts: Some current, and the water can get downright cold!

This swimming hole is actually in the Current River, where Blue Spring runs in. You are swimming between the banks of the river, but it is spring water and it can get COLD! It can be just the thing on a hot Ozarks day, but when you start turning blue you might want to get out.

The spring is a huge outlet of water a couple hundred yards up from the river. Swimming is not allowed in the spring, but it is definitely worth the time and very short hike to go up and see it. Just as the name implies, the spring is a beautiful and brilliant blue color. The average daily flow is about 81 million gallons of bone chilling water.

To reach the parking area from Eminence, Missouri, go east on Highway 106 for 15 miles and turn right onto the gravel road at the "Blue Springs" sign. At 0.1 mile, there is a fork—stay right and follow this road to the parking area.

At the south end of the parking area, you will see the trail leading into the woods. Follow the trail along the riverbank until it turns up the hill. Directly ahead, you will see the trail fork; take the right fork just a few yards to the river. The left fork takes you to the spring, just a short hike away.

Emergency: Shannon County Sheriff, 573–226–3615

Blue Spring Hole, Current River

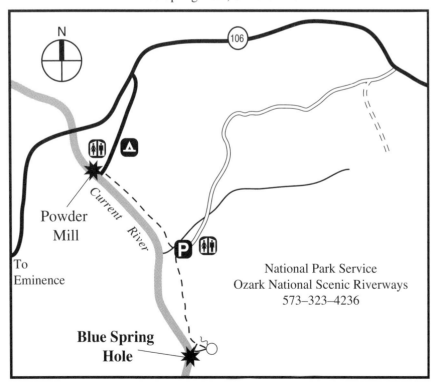

#69 Log Yard

Current River, Shannon County, Missouri

Agency: National Park Service, Ozark National Scenic Riverways
Nearby community or landmark: Eminence, Missouri
GPS: N: 37°06'47" W: 91°07'43"
Access: Vehicle
Day Use Fee: None
Facilities: • camping sites • fire pits • toilets
Activities: • swimming • fishing • canoeing • picnicking • camping
Alerts: None

Log Yard is one of those classic gravel bar swimming holes that is great for a family outing, camping and skipping rocks. Both the gravel bar and swimming hole are large enough to allow plenty of room if busloads of folks show up. While on our trip, Jesse Scribner rated each location on its rock-skipping potential, and Log Yard was near the top of the list.

To reach the gravel bar from Eminence, Missouri, go east on Highway 106 for 16 miles to Highway HH. Go right on Highway HH for 6.2 miles to a "T" intersection, then turn right and go 0.7 mile to the three-way intersection. Take the left road and follow it to the gravel bar. Swim anywhere along the gravel bar.

Emergency: Shannon County Sheriff, 573–226–3615

Log Yard, Current River

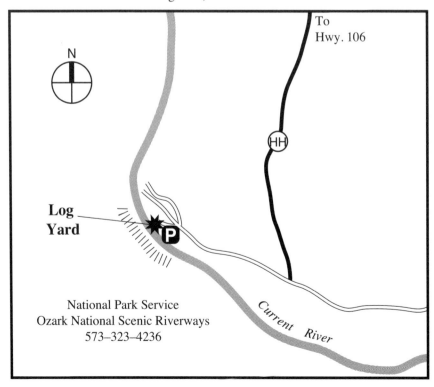

#76 Rocky Falls
Little Rocky Creek, Shannon County, Missouri

Agency: National Park Service, Ozark National Scenic Riverways
Nearby community or landmark: Eminence, Missouri
GPS: N: 37°05'38" W: 91°12'34"
Access: Vehicle and a short walk
Day Use Fee: None
Facilities: • picnic tables • fire pits • permanent chemical toilets • hiking trails • map and information boxes
Activities: • swimming • hiking • picnicking • exploring
Alerts: There are some great rock formations to crawl around on and explore, but be careful. They can become extremely slick, especially when wet.

This is a great spot!! The creek here tumbles down one of the most beautiful cascades in the area and forms a large pool at the bottom. You can bring the family here and spend the entire day swimming, hiking the trails, exploring the gorgeous rocks or just kicking back.

Above the waterfall is a very interesting glade area that classes from colleges throughout Missouri come to study and the geology here is pretty impressive as well. But even if you aren't into the ecology or geology of the place, bring your camera. This is a spectacular spot to burn some film (or digital media).

To find this little slice of heaven, leave Eminence, Missouri, on Highway 106 going east. Go 7.5 miles to Highway H and turn right (south). Follow Highway H for 3.8 miles to Highway NN, where you will turn left. Go 1.9 miles on Highway NN and turn right onto Shannon County Road NN526. Go 0.3 mile and turn left to the parking area. Just follow the trail from the parking area to the swimming hole.

Emergency: Shannon County Sheriff, 573–226–3615

Rocky Falls, Little Rocky Creek

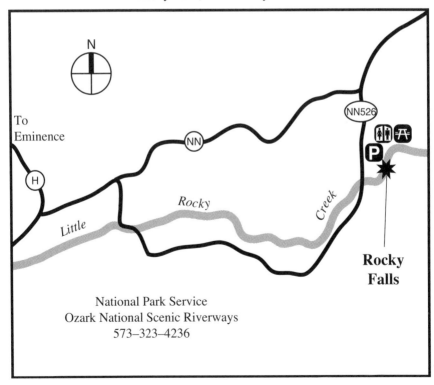

National Park Service
Ozark National Scenic Riverways
573–323–4236

#85 Watercress

Current River, Carter County, Missouri

Agency: U.S. Forest Service, Mark Twain National Forest
Nearby community or landmark: Van Buren, Missouri
GPS: N: 37°00'09" W: 91°01'09"
Access: Vehicle
Day Use Fee: None
Facilities: • picnic areas • pavilions • campsites • boat ramp • water • toilets
• NPS and USFS visitor centers just up the hill
Activities: • swimming • fishing • camping • picnicking
Alerts: Posted signs say to watch for sharp drop-offs and currents, however this is known as a good place to bring kids unless water levels are up.

Watercress is a park on the Current River that is located on the edge of Van Buren, Missouri. It is very easy to access and has become known as a good place for mom and dad to bring the kids to play in the water because there are several areas where it remains shallow for quite a distance from the bank. On the other hand, everyone, parents especially, should watch for quick drop-offs. Don't come here expecting to find a great, out-of-the-way swimming hole, but if the kids are wanting to play in the water or the extended family is wanting to get together for a picnic or cookout, it is worth checking into.

From Highway 60 in Van Buren, Missouri, go north on Business 60 for 0.2 mile to the stop sign and turn right (east); you are still on Business 60. Go another 0.2 mile and turn left at the sign for the Ozark National Scenic Riverways visitor center. Drive past the visitor center and turn left at the "Y" intersection at 0.1 mile, then wind down the hill and into the recreation area. There are several places to park here and you can just look at the river to find the area where you want to play. Or just pick a part of the river that is close to the facilities you have rented for the day or the picnic spot you have occupied.

Emergency: Carter County Sheriff, 573–323–4146

Watercress, Current River

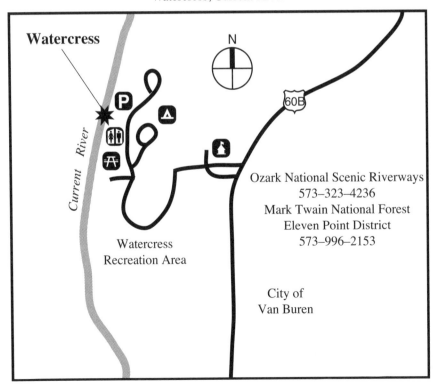

Watercress

N

60B

Current River

Ozark National Scenic Riverways
573–323–4236
Mark Twain National Forest
Eleven Point District
573–996–2153

Watercress
Recreation Area

City of
Van Buren

#51 Big Spring Hole, Current River

Current River, Carter County, Missouri
Agency: National Park Service, Ozark National Scenic Riverways
Nearby community or landmark: Van Buren, Missouri
GPS: N: 36°57'05" W: 90°59'26"
Access: Vehicle
Day Use Fee: None
Facilities: • campgrounds • playground • hiking trails • restrooms • amphitheater • ranger station • lodge • restaurant • gift shop • cabins • pay phone
Activities: • swimming • camping • dining • shopping • picnicking • playing • canoeing • fishing • history • hiking
Alerts: None

First off, I have to start with somewhat of a plug here. In doing this book and all the other time I spend out and about, I have visited many areas within national parks and have spoken to and encountered countless park rangers. The vast majority of the rangers have been great folks and would help in any way they could. Some, of course, were friendlier and more helpful than others, as in any profession. But I must say that the day I drove into Big Spring and started trying to find out information, I encountered, without a doubt, the friendliest and most helpful National Park Ranger I have ever dealt with. Now don't get me wrong, in my old line of work, I have worked with and around some great ones, but Jodi Towery took the cake! My hat is off to Jodi and the picture she paints of our National Park Service!

Now that I got that out of my system… Big Spring is a great place to visit and I would highly recommend it as a place to take the family. It is named after the huge spring that reveals itself there. The largest spring in Missouri puts out an average of 276 million gallons of water a day!

Big Spring is also the site of an old CCC camp. The CCC, or Civilian Conservation Corps, was organized by President Roosevelt in the late 1930's to create jobs and training for young, able-bodied men during the great depression. The workers were first taken to "basic training" by the U.S. Army for a few weeks to get them in shape to do the work that would be asked of them. They were given all their basic needs and actually lived a pretty good life compared to some of the alternatives. They were paid $1 a day, but were required to send most of it home to their families. It did a lot of good for the country and for most of the young men who made the decision to join. The CCC left behind some wonderful things that we still enjoy today. They built numerous cabins and lodges at state parks, dams, bridges and all kinds of projects that are absolute treasures. At Big Spring, there are several CCC cabins available to rent and a large lodge built by the CCC.

To reach Big Spring from Highway 60 in Van Buren, Missouri, go south on Highway 103 for approximately 4.1 miles. You will have passed the entry to Big Spring Park. Cross the bridge and park in the small parking area across from the pavilion by the spring. Follow the trail through the woods a very short distance to the river. This is another of the places where there is no real "hole" to swim in, but there are several places in the park that make nice spots.

Emergency: Carter County Sheriff, 573–323–4510

Big Spring Hole, Current River

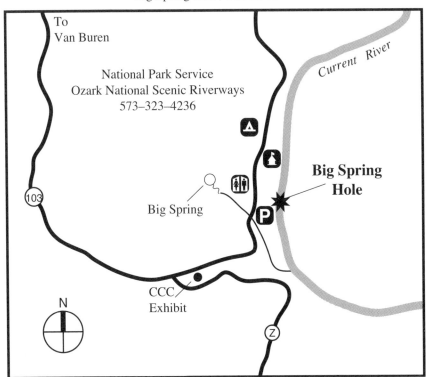

#52 Big Tree

Current River, Carter County, Missouri

Agency: National Park Service, Ozark National Scenic Riverways
Nearby community or landmark: Van Buren, Missouri
GPS: N: 36°55'30" W: 90°54'08"
Access: Vehicle, four-wheel drive sometimes needed
Day Use Fee: Yes
Facilities: • basic campsites • picnic tables • grills • fire pits • lantern poles
Activities: • swimming • fishing • camping • picnicking • canoeing
Alerts: Watch for flooding.

Big Tree is a recreation area that has a few basic campsites and is a kind of out-of-the-way, quiet place. This is the Current River, so again, no big holes, but good water to get wet in. It would also make a nice camp spot if you were looking to get away from the more modern places.

From Highway 60 in Van Buren, Missouri, go south on Highway 103 for 3.8 miles to Highway Z (just past the entrance to Big Spring Park) and turn right (south). Follow Highway Z for 7.4 miles and turn left (east) at the "Big Tree" sign. Follow that 0.5 mile to the recreation area. Just before you get into the recreation area, you will have to cross a small stream. If the water is up and moving very much, think twice about trying to cross it. Additionally, if much rain is in the forecast, this might not be the best place to camp. You might find yourself stranded between two flooded streams with nowhere to go.

Once in the recreation area, swim anywhere that suits your fancy.

Emergency: Carter County Sheriff, 573–323–4510

Big Tree, Current River

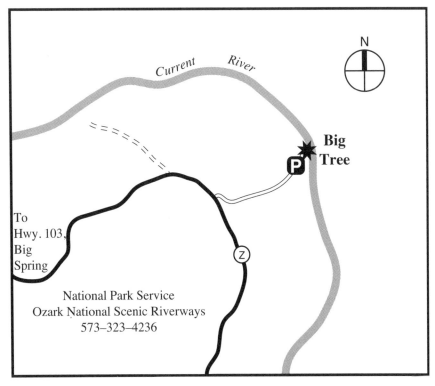

#64 Gooseneck
Current River, Carter County, Missouri

Agency: National Park Service, Ozark National Scenic Riverways
Nearby community or landmark: Van Buren, Missouri
GPS: N: 36°49'06" W: 90°56'51"
Access: Vehicle, but it can get rough
Day Use Fee: None
Facilities: • basic campsites • picnic table • grill • fire pit • lantern pole • boat ramp
Activities: • swimming • fishing • camping • canoeing
Alerts: Pay attention to the currents.

Gooseneck is an out-of-the-way, almost secluded place that is on the very edge of the Ozark National Scenic Riverways. The road in can get rough at times, but it is also fairly easy to access with most vehicles.

As with much of the Current River, there is no real "swimmin' hole" here, but there is some good water, and the location is worth the visit.

To reach Gooseneck from Van Buren, Missouri, go west on Highway 60 for 5.1 miles to Highway C and turn left (south). Go 11.7 miles on Highway C and turn left (east) onto Forest Road 3142/Carter County Road C–10 (the latter turns into Carter County Road C–10A on down the road). Follow that road 6.2 miles to the recreation area. Once you enter the campground, make a right at the sign and fee station and it is another 0.2 mile to the campsites.

Emergency: Carter County Sheriff, 573–323–4510

Gooseneck, Current River

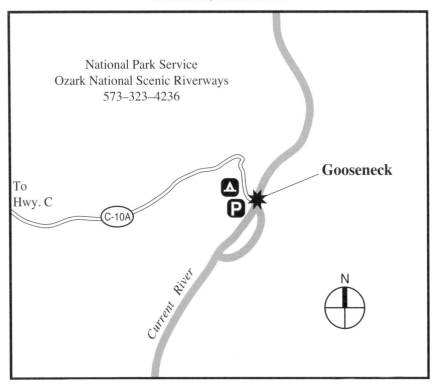

National Park Service
Ozark National Scenic Riverways
573–323–4236

To
Hwy. C

C-10A

Gooseneck

Current River

N

#71 McCormack Lake
McCormack Lake, Oregon County, Missouri

Agency: U.S. Forest Service, Mark Twain National Forest
Nearby community or landmark: Alton, Missouri
GPS: N: 36°49'18" W: 91°21'07"
Access: Vehicle
Day Use Fee: None
Facilities: • basic campsites • picnic tables • benches • toilets • trailhead
Activities: • swimming • fishing • hiking • camping
Alerts: None

McCormack Lake is one of several little jewels of lakes the Forest Service has in this part of Missouri. This one has a trailhead to the Ozark Trail, some camping, picnicking and some benches placed around to just sit and enjoy the wonderful surroundings.

If you leave Alton, Missouri, head north on Highway 19 for 12.9 miles to Forest Road 3155 (there is a McCormack Lake sign there) and turn left. Follow that to the lake. There are two parking areas; the first is at 1.9 miles and the second is at 2.3 miles.

Emergency: Oregon County Sheriff, 417–778–6611

McCormack Lake

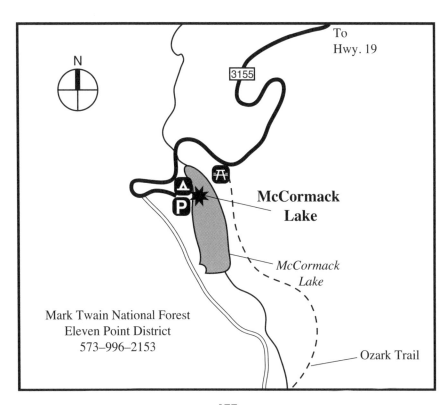

#75 Riverton

Eleven Point River, Oregon County, Missouri

Agency: U. S. Forest Service, Mark Twain National Forest
Nearby community or landmark: Alton, Missouri
GPS: N: 36°38'54" W: 91°12'04"
Access: Vehicle
Day Use Fee: None
Facilities: • picnic areas • grills • toilets • boat ramp
Activities: • swimming • fishing • canoeing • picnicking
Alerts: None

There are actually two access points at Riverton; one is Riverton West and the other, what else? Riverton East. Basically they are accessed on either end of the bridge that spans the Eleven Point River. Riverton East is geared more toward canoe access and boat launching while Riverton West is a picnic area that would be better suited for swimming. What I'll talk about in the directions and descriptions is Riverton West, but to get to Riverton East, just go on across the bridge from Riverton West and take the first left. Then follow the signs to the parking area.

Back to Riverton West: from the intersection of Highways 160 and 19 in Alton, Missouri, go east on Highway 160 for 12.7 miles. Just before crossing the bridge there, you will see a sign for the Riverton Picnic Area. Turn right (south) into the parking area. Just follow the paved path down to the picnic area along the river.

Emergency: Oregon County Sheriff, 417–778–6611

Riverton, Eleven Point River

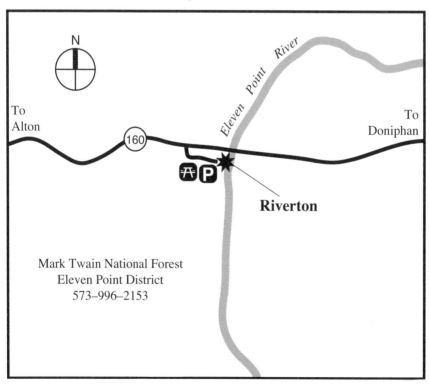

#70 Loggers Lake

Loggers Lake, Shannon County, Missouri

Agency: U.S. Forest Service, Mark Twain National Forest
Nearby community or landmark: Bunker, Missouri
GPS: N: 37°23'23" W: 91°15'36"
Access: Vehicle
Day Use Fee: Yes
Facilities: • campground • picnic area • boat ramp • drinking water • vault toilets
Activities: • swimming • fishing • boating • camping • picnicking
Alerts: None

Loggers Lake is a 22-acre lake near Bunker, Missouri. There are 14 campsites, but no hookups. There are drinking water and vault toilets centrally located in the campground.

From the intersection of Highways 72 and A in Bunker, Missouri, go west on Highway A for 0.2 mile and turn left (south) onto Lincoln Avenue (this will soon turn into Forest Road 2221). Follow that 6.0 miles, staying right at 3.8 miles, and turn left at the campground sign (Forest Road 2193). Reset your trip meter here. Continue on, taking the left at 0.2 mile, to 0.8 mile where you will find a "Y" in the road and directional signs. Go right as indicated by the swimming area sign and parking is just down the hill. Swim beside the parking area.

Emergency: Shannon County Sheriff, 573–226–3615

Loggers Lake

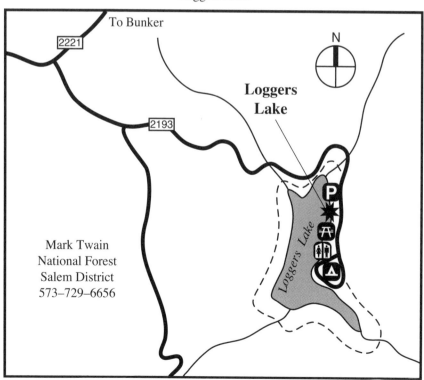

#66 Johnson's Shut-Ins

East Fork of the Black River, Reynolds County, Missouri

Agency: Missouri Department of Natural Resources
Nearby community or landmark: Ironton, Missouri
GPS: N: 37°32'22" W: 90°50'17"
Access: Short hike to swimming hole from campground
Day Use Fee: None
Facilities: • campground • picnic areas • picnic shelters • pavilion • vault toilets • flushing restrooms • bathhouse with showers • hiking trails • horse trails • visitors center/store • amphitheater • playground • pay phone
Activities: • swimming • fishing • camping • horseback riding • playground activities • picnicking • rock climbing and rappelling (seasonal, by permit only) • hiking • interpretive programs
Alerts: Dangerous cliffs and rocks near the swimming hole—watch your kids!

O.K., this one takes the cake in Missouri. It is really something to see. It was voted the best swimming hole in Missouri awhile back in a *Rural Missouri* reader's poll. The only real problem is that it can get very crowded.

State Park officials limit how many folks can be in the park at once and although that number is pretty high, I have heard stories of waiting for hours to get in. I would assume that is more the case on busy weekends and holidays. If you do come, when you get in, it is worth it.

The East Fork of the Black River cuts its way through, over and around some spectacular rock formations, creating hundreds of waterfalls and cascades. It then spills into a nice swimming hole before again making its way through more rocks and crashing over a huge waterfall. If you visit this one, go ahead and hike up past the swimming hole and check out the view of the river below you. Many parts of the cliffs here are off limits without a permit. This is for everyone's safety, but the water below you is absolutely beautiful. Rock climbing and rappelling are available on a seasonal basis, by permit.

To reach this natural water park from Ironton, Missouri, go north on Highway 21 for approximately 3.5 miles (Highway 21 makes a 90 degree left turn at the four-way intersection at 3.0 miles). At 3.5 miles turn left (south) on Highway N by a couple of convenience stores. Follow Highway N for 12.8 miles and turn left at the entrance to the park. Follow the signs on the main road to the ranger station and store. Park in the day use area and follow the trail approximately 0.25 mile to the swimming hole. The trail is all paved or boardwalk and is easy hiking.

Emergency: Reynolds County Sheriff, 573–648–2491

Johnson's Shut-Ins, East Fork of the Black River

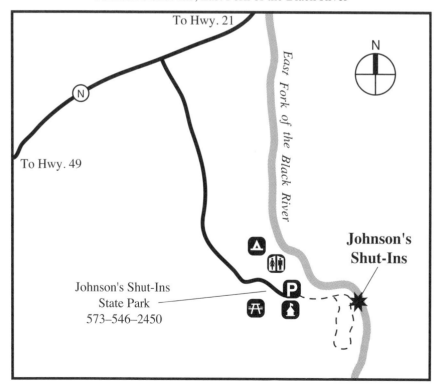

#60 Crane Lake
Crane Lake, Iron County, Missouri

Agency: U.S. Forest Service, Mark Twain National Forest
Nearby community or landmark: Ironton, Missouri
GPS: N: 37°25'19" W: 90°37'18"
Access: Vehicle
Day Use Fee: None
Facilities: • boat ramp • picnic area • hiking trails • toilets
Activities: • swimming • fishing • hiking • boating (electric motors only)
Alerts: None

This is yet another of Missouri's jewels in the forest. It is one of the lakes within the Mark Twain National Forest for which the main form of recreation is fishing, but it is also a good place to cool off. This lake, of about 100 acres, would be a great place for the family to come to so dad could fish, mom could read her book at the picnic tables and the kids could splash and swim. Just remember if you haul the boat up here to fish out of, only electric motors are allowed. So you'll have to leave the 250 Mercury at home.

From the intersection of Highways 34 and 49 in Piedmont, Missouri, go north on Highway 49 for 25.9 miles to Iron County Road 124 and go right (east) 3.6 miles to the cross roads (Iron County Road 131). Go right (south) and follow that road 0.2 mile to the parking area.

Emergency: Iron County Sheriff, 573–546–7321

Crane Lake

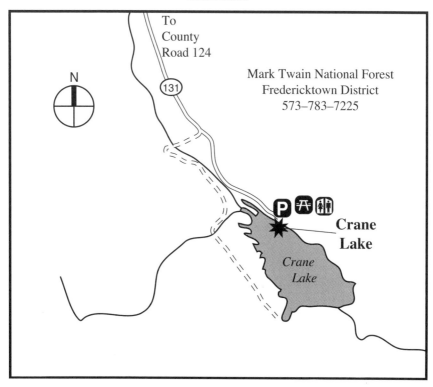

To
County
Road 124

131

N

Mark Twain National Forest
Fredericktown District
573–783–7225

P 🏕️ 🚻 **Crane Lake**

Crane Lake

#59 Castor River Shut-Ins
Castor River, Madison County, Missouri

Agency: Missouri Department of Conservation
Nearby community or landmark: Fredericktown, Missouri
GPS: N: 37°34'04" W: 90°08'54"
Access: Short Hike
Day Use Fee: None
Facilities: None
Activities: • swimming • fishing • hiking • hunting
Alerts: Somewhat isolated and the rocks can be slick and dangerous.

What a neat place this is! It is managed by the Missouri Department of Conservation and actually lies within the Amidon Memorial Conservation Area. The Castor River cuts its way through a gorgeous section of pink-colored granite, causing small cascades, pools, swirls and other features that really add to the character of the place. In a way it reminds me of Johnson's Shut-Ins, except smaller and more peaceful. I have been told it gets a little crowded on occasion, but nothing like its bigger and more famous contemporary. The rocks here can get pretty slick and treacherous when wet so be careful and watch the kids.

From the intersection of Highways 72 and Z in downtown Fredericktown, Missouri, go east on Highway 72 for 2.6 miles to Highway J and turn left (northeast). Reset here. Go 4.2 miles and turn right (south) onto Highway W and reset again. At 1.1 miles Highway W will turn into Madison County Road 208 — go left here (no odometer reset needed), then at 2.2 miles turn left onto Madison County Road 253 at the Department of Conservation sign. It is another 0.8 mile to the parking area.

There is a nice and very well-maintained trail that leaves the parking area and goes around the end of the field and into the woods. Follow that a few hundred yards to the river and swimming hole.

Emergency: Madison County Sheriff, 573–783–2234

Castor River Shut-Ins, Castor River

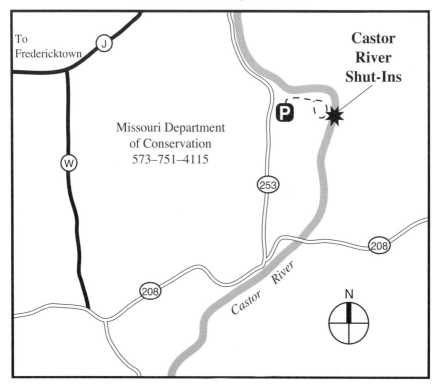

#67 Lake Boutin

Lake Boutin, Cape Girardeau County, Missouri

Agency: Missouri Department of Natural Resources, State Parks
Nearby community or landmark: Cape Girardeau, Missouri
GPS: N: 37°27'18" W: 89°29'08"
Access: Vehicle
Day Use Fee: None
Facilities: • campgrounds • picnic areas • swimming area • showers • restrooms • laundry • scenic overlooks • visitor center • hiking trails • dump stations • boat ramps • playgrounds • pavilions • horse trails • pay phone
Activities: • swimming • fishing • hiking • camping • picnicking • boating
Alerts: None

Lake Boutin is a neat little lake at the Trail of Tears State Park, north of Cape Girardeau, Missouri. This is a first-class state park with some unique terrain, great facilities and fascinating history. Some of the park literature and the website states that some of the terrain is more like that found in the Appalachians than the Ozarks. With the sharp topographical features and the variety of the trees, it did look very "Appalachianesque." (It actually does remind me of the Appalachians, but really, I just wanted an excuse to use the new word I had made up.)

And the history, of course, is from the infamous forced migration of the Native Americans (mainly Cherokee at this state park) from their eastern homelands to what is now Oklahoma. Floating ice on the Mississippi River put a halt to attempted river crossings there and forced the travelers to set up camps on both sides of the river, many camped at what is now the park. Conditions were horrendous, with freezing cold, starvation, and disease constant companions. Many died at the impromptu camps. It has been estimated that more that 4,000 Cherokees died on the march, nearly 20 percent of the total population. In addition to the great swimming and other outdoor related activities here, the historical significance is worth a visit.

To reach the park from Interstate 55 take Exit 105/Highway 61 to Fruitland, Missouri, and go east 0.8 mile to Highway 177 and turn right (still east). Follow Highway 177 (staying right at 7.3 miles will keep you on Highway 177) until you find the left turn onto Hill Road at 10.2 miles—you should see a sign pointing to the lake. Follow Hill Road and go straight at the stop sign. At 0.5 mile turn right into the parking lot.

If you are in Cape Girardeau (we'll start from downtown at the intersection of Broadway and Main), go north on Highway 177 for 12 miles to Hill Road and follow the above directions. Buoys just below the parking lot mark off the swimming area.

While you are this close, downtown Cape Girardeau is a neat place to visit. The downtown has a lot of character and the bridges over the Mississippi are great. You can find out more about the state park on the web at:

www.mostateparks.com/trailoftears.htm
Emergency: 911 or Cape Girardeau County Sheriff, 573–243–3551

Lake Boutin

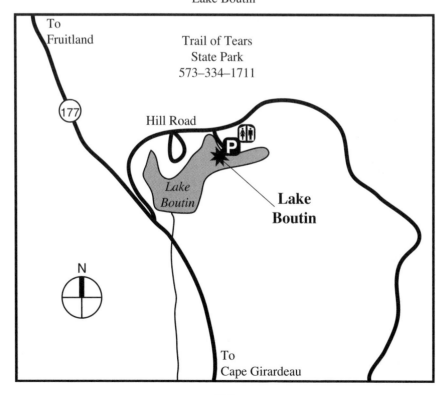

To
Fruitland

Trail of Tears
State Park
573–334–1711

177

Hill Road

P

*Lake
Boutin*

**Lake
Boutin**

N

To
Cape Girardeau

About the Author

Glenn Wheeler is a freelance writer and photographer who makes his home near Harrison, Arkansas, along with his wife Stacey, their daughter Elizabeth and their son, Zane. Glenn was born and raised in the beautiful Ozark Mountains near the Buffalo National River and has always loved the area for its beauty, its charm and its people.

He began photographing it as a boy and eventually turned it into a career. He later began writing about the area as well, and after several years with a "real job" he retired and was able to begin chasing his dream. His work has appeared in numerous magazines, books, newspapers, brochures, tour guides and websites and his prints hang on walls of homes and offices in several states and on two continents.

He is currently working on his next book project, *The Vanishing Ozarks*, photographing everywhere he gets the chance, leading or helping with photography workshops and trips, teaching photography classes for various schools and organizations, writing the occasional magazine article, selling fine art prints of his work, serving as President of the Photography Club of the Ozarks, worshiping the ground Stacey walks on, thinking Elizabeth hung the moon, and trying to keep Zane out of trouble. In his free time he likes to—who are we kidding?—he doesn't have any free time!

You can learn more about Glenn, his family, his work and his projects by visiting his website **www.GlennWheeler.com**.

The "Four Wheelers"—Glenn, Zane, Beth, and Stacey, photo by Jesse Scribner

Books by Tim Ernst Publishing

SWIMMING HOLES OF THE OZARKS GUIDE (Glenn Wheeler)
Maps, photos, directions, and GPS info. for 85 great swimming holes
5.5" x 8.5", 192 pages, $19.95
ARKANSAS WATERFALLS GUIDE (Tim Ernst)
Maps, color photos, descriptions, & GPS info. for more than 200 great waterfalls
6" x 9", 224 pages, $22.95
ARKANSAS NATURE LOVER'S GUIDE (Tim Ernst)
Maps, color photos, descriptions, & GPS info. for 101 great scenic areas
6" x 9", 224 pages, $22.95
ARKANSAS HIKING TRAILS GUIDE (Tim Ernst)
Maps and descriptions of 78 major trails in the state
6" x 9", 192 pages, $19.95
BUFFALO RIVER HIKING TRAILS GUIDE (Tim Ernst)
Maps and descriptions of over 30 trails in the river area
5.5" x 8.5", 136 pages, $19.95
OUACHITA TRAIL GUIDE (Tim Ernst)
Complete guide to the longest trail in the region. 10 maps and elevation profiles
5.5" x 8.5", 136 pages, $19.95
OZARK HIGHLANDS TRAIL GUIDE (Tim Ernst)
The definitive guide to this fabulous 165–mile trail.13 maps, 9 elevation profiles
5.5" x 8.5", 136 pages, $19.95
ARKANSAS DAYHIKES FOR KIDS & FAMILIES GUIDE (Pam Ernst)
Maps and descriptions of 89 great easy dayhikes in the state
6" x 9", 128 pages, $19.95
ARKANSAS WILDFLOWERS GUIDE (Don Kurz)
423 color photos, color-coded descriptions of more than 400 species
6" x 9", 256 pages, $22.95
ILLINOIS WILDFLOWERS GUIDE (Don Kurz)
429color photos, color-coded descriptions of more than 400 species
6" x 9", 256 pages, $24.95
MISSOURI'S NATURAL WONDERS GUIDE (Don Kurz)
Maps, color photos, descriptions, & GPS info. for 100 great scenic areas
6" x 9", 128 pages, $22.95

These guidebooks, plus a selection of coffee-table picture books and Arkansas
calendars can be found at your local bookstore, outdoor store, or park visitor center.
Visit the web page below to order all of these publications, plus fine art prints and
photo workshops by Tim Ernst; also find the largest selection of Arkansas outdoor
guidebooks and maps available anywhere:

www.TimErnst.com

Legend For All Maps

P Parking Area

✳ Swimming Hole Location

////// Bluff

- - - - Trail

~~~ Creek, Stream, River

ℹ **🚻** Visitor Center, Restroom

⛺ **⛱** Campground, Picnic Area

⟨71⟩ Paved Highway

㉓ �341 State/County Road

[1003] Gravel Forest Road

▬▬▬ Paved Road

═══ Gravel Road

= = = = Jeep Road

▭ Building

ᕤ ⅄ † Spring, Cave/Mine, Cemetery

MISSOURI OZARKS _{page 114}

24 thru 48 are on
Buffalo River map
on page 62

ARKANSAS OZARKS _{page 14}

PUBLICATIONS BY TIM ERNST

Arkansas Waterfalls guidebook
Arkansas Nature Lover's guidebook
Arkansas Hiking Trails guidebook
Arkansas Dayhikes For Kids guidebook
Buffalo River Hiking Trails guidebook
Ozark Highlands Trail guidebook
Ouachita Trail guidebook
Arkansas Greatest Hits picture book
Arkansas Splendor picture book
Arkansas Beauty picture book
Arkansas In My Own Backyard picture book
A Rare Quality Of Light picture book
Buffalo River Beauty picture book
Arkansas Nightscapes picture book
Arkansas Landscapes II picture book
Arkansas Portfolio III picture book
Arkansas Autumn picture book
Arkansas Wildlife picture book
Arkansas Landscapes picture book
Buffalo River Dreams picture book
Arkansas Waterfalls picture book
Arkansas Portfolio II picture book
Arkansas Wilderness picture book
Buffalo River Wilderness picture book
Arkansas Spring picture book
Wilderness Reflections picture book
Arkansas Portfolio picture book
The Search For Haley
The Cloudland Journal

We stock the most complete selection available of wilderness maps,
Trails Illustrated maps of the Buffalo River, Ozark Highlands Trail
maps, Ouachita Trail maps, canoe guides, and other outdoor publications of Arkansas and the Buffalo River.

For autographed copies or info on any of our products contact:
Tim Ernst Publishing
online store: www.TimErnst.com
870–446–3282

LEGEND FOR ALL MAPS

———————	Main Trails—Described Route	████████	Paved Highway
– – – – –	Other Trail or Bushwhack Route	════════	Dirt /Gravel Road
··········	Old River Horse Trail	= = = =	Jeep Road
⊖——P 1.8	Mileage Between Points (Longer Trails Only)	⌒⌒	Rivers/Streams/Creeks
P	Trailhead Parking	🛡59	Federal Highway
🅿	Campground	88	State Highway
🅰		25 9560	County Road
🎋	Day Use/Picnic Area	1003	Forest Road
🔧	Historical Site	\\\\|||||/////	Bluffs/Mountaintop
❓	Ranger Station	Oᵣ Y ✗	Spring, Cave, Mine
♿	Wheelchair Access		
⌁ ✝	Church, Cemetery		Wilderness Area
✳	Point of Interest		

Buffalo National River Area

Arkansas.
THE NATURAL STATE

Call 1–800–NATURAL
for a free Vacation Planning Kit.